RUSSIA:
A JOURNEY TO THE ARCTIC

THE ADVENTURES OF LIVING INSIDE
A REMOTE SIBERIAN WEATHER STATION &
THE EXPERIENCES HE HAD ALONG THE WAY

LARRY RITCO

 FriesenPress

Suite 300 - 990 Fort St
Victoria, BC, V8V 3K2
Canada

www.friesenpress.com

Copyright © 2019 by Larry Ritco
First Edition — 2019

ISBN
978-1-5255-4393-7 (Hardcover)
978-1-5255-4394-4 (Paperback)
978-1-5255-4395-1 (eBook)

1. *Travel, Russia*

Distributed to the trade by The Ingram Book Company

TABLE OF CONTENTS

BOOKS BY LARRY RITCO

Ask your bookseller for the books you have missed.

...Okay, I have to admit that this is just the first
book I have written. ...But stay tuned!

To Gay,
To the sweetest, most charming
lady.
Lots of love!
Larry Ritco

PROJECT PERSONNEL AND PEOPLE WE MET

Bob Forsyth (Canadian)	Observation team leader- Flox weather station, Baydaratskaya Bay
John Fitcher (Canadian)	Observer- Flox weather station, B. B.
Ray Hunt (Canadian)	Observer- Victoria weather station, Baydaratskaya Bay
Larry Ritco (Canadian)	Laboratory observer- Victoria weather station, B. B.
Peter 1 (Dutch)	Observer- Victoria weather station, B. B.
Peter 2 (Dutch)	Observer- Flox weather station, B. B.
Alex Costin (Canadian)	Initial logistics coordinator- HBT Agra, Calgary office, Calgary, Can.
Jim Oswell (Canadian)	Engineer- HBT Agra, Calgary and Heerema office, Leiden, Holland
Al Hanna (Canadian)	Engineer- HBT Agra, Calgary office
Derick (J.F.) Nixon (Canadian)	Permafrost specialist consultant- Calgary
Ard Doorduyn (Dutch)	Observation team coordinator (OTC)- Heerema office, Leiden, H.
Ron Aartsee (Dutch)	Logistics coordinator (LC)- Heerema office, Leiden, H.
Sasha (Russian)	Driver- Heerema, Moscow, Russia
Nadisha (Nedella) (Russian)	Host- Amiga company, Murmansk, Russia

Alexander (Russian)	Host- Amiga company, Murmansk, R.
Alexander Zubov (Russian)	Director Consulor- Amiga company representing Gazprom
Lela (Russian)	Interpreter- Nadym, Russia
Arthur (Russian)	Interpreter- Victoria weather station and throughout the travels
Eva (Russian)	Restaurant 65 host- Nadym, Russia
Andre (Russian)	Drilling crew, chess champion (at times) of the Arctic Circle, Victoria weather Station, B. B.
Mesha (Michael) (Russian)	Shotgun holder, polar bear security & DCP trouble shooter, Victoria weather station, B. B. (also a great Russian story teller)
Alex (Russian)	Cook- Victoria weather station, B. B.
Mr. Famienko (Russian)	Amiga company- representing Gazprom
Michael (Russian)	Interpreter/teacher- Labytnangi, Russia
Roman Kolbergenov (Russian)	Laboratory manager- Obskaya, Russia
Tatyana Hefedova (Russian)	Assistant laboratory manager- Obskaya, R.
Ura (Russian)	Laboratory technician- Obskaya, R.
Sasha (Russian)	Laboratory technician- Obskaya, R.
Anton (Russian)	Laboratory technician- Obskaya, R.
Nick (Russian)	Larry's escort from the laboratory to Salekhard Airport, Russia
Lidea (Russian)	Secretary- Heerema office, Moscow,
Sergei (Russian)	Engineer and escort to foreign embassy, Heerema office, Moscow
Marian (Dutch)	Secretary- Heerema office, Leiden, Holland
Jose Duriex (Dutch)	Secretary- Heerema office, Leiden, H.
	&
Gypsy (Unknown nationality)	- the castaway dog and official greeter of Victoria weather station, Baydaratskaya Bay, Russia

MAPS
OUR JOURNEY

Route to Baydaratskaya Bay, Russia

Closeup of Baydaratskaya Bay

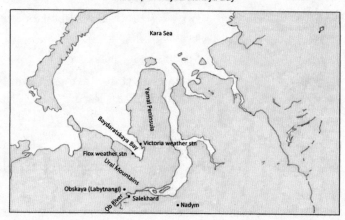

PREFACE

When Alex Costin approached me at work in the winter of 1993 to ask me if I wanted to go to Russia, I was firmly entrenched with living my life with my well-established routines. I was content, but was I happy? Probably not, but I was safe. I told him no, but thankfully, he persisted, and I reconsidered. After weighing the options and considering the positives versus the negatives, I thought, "Why not?"

This trip to Russia gave me the opportunity to go outside my comfort zone, with its nine-to-five, five-day workweek lifestyle, and into the unknown. I said yes and I will never regret it.

The time I spent in Russia will always remain a special part of my scrapbook of lifetime memories. This opportunity allowed me to seize the moment and broaden my horizons. It allowed me to have adventures I never dreamed possible. The experience, including the successes and mistakes, added up to an abundance of memories, good and bad, that I shall have for the rest of my life. I can even look back to one of the loneliest times in my life and remember it fondly. I was on an empty road in the middle of the night with a stranger in Labytnangi, and things looked bleak-but more on that later.

If you ever get the opportunity to go outside your comfort zone, seize the moment, as I did, and go for it. Live an adventure! You will never regret it.

CHAPTER 1
OPPORTUNITY COMES KNOCKING

Wednesday April 27, 1994. 5:14pm. Calgary, Alberta.
Day 1

So this is finally it. After numerous delays, we are finally on our way to Russia. We had our final briefing this morning, received our SOS card, and took a taxi from the company to the airport. We had a huge amount of luggage with us—parkas, mukluks, sleeping bags, coats—all in preparation for a cold Siberian winter. Then we found out it's only about -5C there.

Our flight goes from Calgary-Vancouver-Frankfurt-Moscow-Murmansk-site (or a city near the site) where we will probably be helicoptered in, since the roads in the last week or so are closed due to thaw conditions.

I am sitting in the Vancouver airport passenger lounge writing this diary, waiting to board Lufthansa flight 1072 to Frankfurt, West Germany. Departure time on the Boeing 747 is 4:55pm. I arrived one and a half hours ago from my home base in Calgary, Alberta. My so-called "boring life" has been forced out of its comfort zone and will be transformed by a new adventure that will take me to the far north in the Siberian Russian Arctic.

Next to me, sprawled out over several seats with their massive amount of luggage and carry-ons on the floor, are my three Canadian co-workers. Bob Forsythe—mustached, baby-faced, a full 6 feet 10 inches and 265 pounds, with body fat measured in ounces—sits across from me, grinning. Our nickname for him is The Friendly Giant, after the popular Canadian children's program featuring Robert Hommes. Bob, in his mid-thirties, is the leader of our group.

He will coordinate our activities and observations in the field relating to the work project.

A couple seats to Bob's right, amidst coats and jackets, sits Ray Hunt. He is bent over, writing little things in his diary. In his mid-fifties, he is bearded and has thinning blond-red hair. He will be my roommate throughout most of the trip. I have known him for many years, since we have worked together on many projects at HBT Agra, our engineering company. He would bring the soil samples in from the field, and I would run laboratory tests on them. Throughout this trip, I was to get along with him quite well, not only because he is a quiet person, but also because he doesn't snore. Thankfully, the few words he muttered in his sleep were often muffled by his thick beard and mustache.

To my right is John Fitcher from Lethbridge, Alberta. He works at the HBT Agra sister company there. Rugged, hardheaded, and big-nosed, John is in his mid-thirties as well. I only know him from a few of the small inter-office projects that we have worked on. He sits there, looking straight ahead, contemplating life (or perhaps ogling a pretty female traveller walking through the distant concourse). We are part of a six-man observation team that will oversee a drilling program on Baydaratskaya Bay in northern Russia. Two Dutch personnel from the Heerema engineering company will join us in Moscow to complete the team.

As I pause in my writings, I sit back, close my eyes, and reminisce about why I decided to take this trip to Russia in the first place. Why on earth would anybody volunteer to go to the Siberian Arctic in the middle of winter to live and work at a remote, primitive weather station, where the nearest town is hundreds of kilometers away? The only access in is by helicopter, or perhaps a reindeer sled driven by a local herder. Temperatures in the winter of -40 are not uncommon. The food will be basic, and a primitive outhouse will be the only toilet facilities. Modern amenities, such as television and radio, are non-existent. Polar bears are known to lurk outside the camp.

Siberia, by its broadest definition, means "North Asia." It was here that *Katorga*, penal labor, was instituted during the seventeenth century. I just hope that during my stay here, I don't accidentally lose my passport and visa and end up disappearing into one of the chain gangs to develop my rock-breaking skills. Just the word "Siberia" sends shivers up most people's spines. Here I am, living in one of the richest countries in the world, volunteering to go to one of the coldest and remotest places on earth. "Why?" I ask myself.

Perhaps it's the images of tall, beautiful Russian ladies wearing mink coats and fur Shapka Ushankas on their heads, the ones you often see strutting down the fashion walkways of London, Paris, and Milan. Perhaps the charm is found in its romance portrayed in the movie Dr. Zhivago. The movie shows the beauty, loneliness, and the intricate relationships that its lead actor, Omar Shariff, goes through in his conflicted life and love for his country and female companions.

The word "Zhivago" is a Church Slavonic name meaning "the living" or "life." Maybe in some ways, it's symbolic of my journey of trying to live life to the fullest.

I think in the end, though, it was simply that I was presented an opportunity, and I chose to say yes.

— * —

It started with "HBT Agra wins Siberian Contract"

"Calgary energy firm HBT Agra Ltd has a foot in the door to one of Eurasia's largest petroleum projects, a series of 2,500 kilometer natural gas pipelines from Siberia to Central Europe" (business section heading and quotation from the Calgary Herald, December 14, 1993).

The article goes on to talk about how the company's participation involves designing a trench for two 48" gas pipelines on the seabed of the seventy-kilometer wide Baydaratskaya Bay. Gazprom, one of Russia's largest energy companies, plans to build these pipelines.

About a month before this article came out, I knew we had won this contract through our company news magazine, but didn't think much about it. No big deal. It didn't involve me, as I had been working in the soils laboratory for fourteen years doing various jobs. I did lab tests, computer work, billings, and oversaw operations—everything but actually being classified as a manager. Much of my work came from Alberta's booming economy, with its vibrant oil and gas energy sector leading the way, causing the expansion and growth throughout the province. I had never been on an overseas project, but this international project would soon change all that and consume my thoughts over the next few months. My life would become much more enriched as I was to meet, and work alongside, many wonderful people. Although our company, HBT Agra, is based in Canada, with its headquarters here in Calgary, it does have an international flavour, with many overseas offices. It is involved in major projects throughout the construction, environmental, and energy sectors, the latter of which comes into play here.

— * —

November 1993 (one month earlier).

I am sitting at my computer desk, plotting and graphing sieve analysis results from earlier tests I had performed during the day. Our field boss, Gerry Schaeffer, would whistle or clear his throat before coming up behind you. My other boss, Gary Wostradowski, on the other hand, would sneak up behind me to see if I was working. Of course, he would always do this after a hectic period when I'm just trying to catch my breath. This time, though, he doesn't seem to care that I'm not working.

"Larry," he says. "How would you like to go to Russia and be a laboratory observer for a few months?" Whoa! That was unexpected, and not just because he wasn't concerned whether I was working or not. I was flabbergasted and elated, but reality soon set in. I quickly pondered this far-fetched idea.

My first grade teacher foreshadowed my decision-making ability when she wrote, "Larry plods along like the perpetual tortoise. Out of forty-one quizzes, Larry got 10 of 10 right on 37 of them." I didn't take her comments as something derogatory, but rather, as something positive. She, in her astuteness, really did understand how I think! Often people get the answer long before I do. I like to circle around the problem and analyze it from all angles before I make my final decision. She could see that that is how I think. I still consider her comments as one of the best a teacher has ever given me, and she still ranks high, perhaps number one, in my favourite teachers.

"Are you interested?" Gary continued.

"What does it entail?"

I already knew it concerned the pipeline project, but didn't know much about the details.

"They are doing a drilling program. We are sending a small team to observe, and we need a laboratory observer to do that." He continued to update me, but for the most part, I already knew what my answer would be. Since this would involve working on the Sabbath (Saturday), which I faithfully kept, and which Gary knew about, I politely told him I wasn't interested for that reason. He thought that might be my answer, but had to ask me anyways to confirm. He went back to his office.

Throughout the day, I thought about that missed opportunity, but wasn't overly fussed. Our Edmonton office had lots of experienced personnel that could fill the job nicely.

Over the next few weeks, I didn't hear too much about the project and assumed the position was filled. Little did I know, no one in Edmonton was interested. Unlike me, they all had families and kids and didn't want to go overseas. This is where Alex Costin stepped in.

Alex, about sixty years of age and of Romanian descent, was a geotechnical engineer that had worked for the company for many years. He was rugged and athletic for his age, and enjoyed rock climbing as a hobby. I had worked for him on occasions on small field and lab projects. Alex had been selected to be the logistics coordinator representing HBT Agra for this project. His job was to not only oversee the initial planning for us, but also be a liaison between Gazprom and ourselves, and ensure that the Russians were doing their part in the preparations. One of his duties was to ensure that everyone working on the project had all the necessary items, including winter gear, parkas, mukluks, sleeping bags, sunglasses (to prevent snow blindness), small tools, notepads, cameras, toilet paper, and personal items. Then, there was all the paperwork that needed to be filled out: visas, passports, SOS emergency cards, emergency phone numbers, wills, and airline tickets. Most of this had to be done weeks in advance. He also had to arrange first aid training courses and winter arctic survival courses, specifically geared to the environment and nature of our work. Last but not least, he had to ensure everyone had the required vaccination shots.

With his contacts with Gazprom, Alex was to work out the details concerning our salaries, overtime, travel pay, and what currency we would be paid in. Then he needed to confirm that the food and living quarters were adequate at the sites, and lodgings, air, and ground transportation on the way to the site had been prearranged.

Once all this was taken care of, and we were on our way *physically*, his job would essentially be over. Jim Oswell, an engineer from the HBT Agra Calgary office, then stationed in Leiden, Holland, would take over. Jim's role would be limited for us, as most of our engineering directions and questions would be done through the Heerema office and their personnel. Nonetheless, Bob Forsythe, our leader in the field, would keep Jim updated on the drilling and laboratory program throughout our stay. Jim would also be our Canadian representative if we were to encounter any awkward or unsatisfactory situations, and would be the emergency contact person if a personal issue should arise from back home. Later, I was to develop a deeper respect for both Jim and Alex. I saw their kindness and selflessness in action.

At this point, Alex was still pursuing the possibility of having me on the project as the laboratory observer. He approached Gary again to confirm that he still had his approval, if he could convince me to go. Gary reaffirmed. The biggest issue was still the Sabbath. In early December, Alex came to me directly.

"Larry," he said, with his heavy accent. "We still need someone to go to Russia as a laboratory observer." Gary had already told him where I stood concerning my faith.

"If I can make arrangements that you won't have to work on Saturdays, would you be interested in going?"

Wow! Now this was getting interesting. This presented a completely new ballgame. Some serious thinking would have to be done here. What were the pros and cons? What was stopping me from going? It always seems that a person goes through the negative options first, before they even start thinking of the positives.

After a bit more discussion concerning the details of the project, I answered non-committedly that yes, I would be interested.

"I will talk to the people at Gazprom and see what we can arrange. I'll keep in touch."

"Good enough," I replied.

Alex headed back to his office in the building next door. I sat, rather stunned at what had just transpired. I was surprised that I had told him I was considering going. This was a big step for me, to step out of my comfort zone.

My mind was racing. What would I need to prepare? Were my bills paid? What would I need to buy and get done ahead of time? I began to feel excited.

A couple of weeks later, Alex gave me an update on what the Russian government proposed. Unlike the others on our team, whose pay will include overtime and travel pay, I would be paid only for the days I actually worked. Each weekend, on Friday nights, I would be helicoptered from the site to the nearby town. I would have the weekends off, but without pay. Then, on Sunday nights, I would be flown back to the site and work the next five days. I was happy with that arrangement. The money issue didn't really bother me. I didn't mind not being paid like everyone else. I thanked Alex and told him I was looking forward to being on the project. To me, this was an opportunity of a lifetime. I was excited to experience something that not many people can say they've done. The travel, Russia, Siberia, the Arctic Circle, and a remote weather station all intrigued me to no end. I would have gone without a salary, as long as my expenses were paid!

— * —

This was it! I was going to Russia! I was overjoyed. Alex did a wonderful job, and I was very appreciative of what he had done for me—and he wasn't finished yet. Without telling me at the time, he got up early the next morning to phone Gazprom in Russia and tell them it was unacceptable for me, the laboratory observer not to be paid seven days a week, including overtime and travel pay, like everybody else on the team, regardless of having the weekends off. Eventually, Alex got his way and they agreed to his terms. He told me the next day about his discussions with them, and of course, I was even more elated, and impressed with what he had done for me. That extra effort he made on my behalf was part of what makes Alex so special.

A few years later, when he retired, he came to the laboratory to say his final goodbye to me. Before I could thank him for being such a good person to work for, he stopped me cold.

"No. I want to say something first. You are one of the nicest people I have ever worked with. You are a good worker and easy to get along with, and I enjoyed working with you."

I returned my compliments to him, telling him what a joy it was to work for him as well, but somehow it seemed lame in comparison. It really was Alex who deserved the accolades. He was a great man and one of the nicest people I have ever worked for. Because of my simple commitment to keeping the Sabbath, Alex did everything he could to ensure that I would be accommodated. He worked hard behind the scenes and I admired him because he stood up and respected my Christian faith.

CHAPTER 2
PROJECT OVERVIEW AND PREPARATIONS

In the far north of western Siberia, the Ural Mountains and Yamal Peninsula are home to some of the world's largest oil and gas fields. Gazprom had plans to build a set of pipelines from there to Europe. Formed in 1989 and headquartered in Moscow, Gazprom is a public joint company and one of the largest in Russia.

Heerema, a Dutch engineering firm, was employed through Gazprom's subsidiary, Amiga, to assist in the design and engineering of one of the most difficult aspects of the pipeline: the crossing of Baydaratskaya Bay. The bay area suffers harsh weather conditions, especially in winter, and despite its relatively shallow depth of about thirty meters, the bay itself has complex soil conditions. Heerema hired us, HBT Agra, as subcontractors because of our expertise with permafrost.

The $500,000 contract involved a combination of environmental studies, an observation team to observe a drilling and laboratory program, and the engineering support and design of the pipeline crossing of Baydaratskaya Bay. This bay is seventy kilometers wide at its widest, and thirty kilometers at its narrowest.

Two drilling programs, one at each end of the narrowest crossing, would be carried out by a Russian contractor along the proposed pipeline route. Laboratory tests would follow. The aforementioned four Canadians and two Dutch would make up the observation team.

The observation team's responsibilities were to observe, take photographs, write notes, and ask questions. They could not interfere with the work project, nor offer advice or criticism. The results of the findings would be written in two reports, one on the drilling program, and one on the laboratory program. Included in these reports would be the quality and condition of the (Russian) contractor's equipment and machinery, the quality of their work, expertise level, what standards they used, and how they compared to North American standards. Bob Forsythe would write the drilling report, and I would write the laboratory report. They would be sent to Gazprom, Heerema, and the Calgary offices to help the engineering teams in their design of the crossing. A main concern was whether the bay where the pipeline(s) would cross was in the permafrost. This was crucial in the design aspect.

Dr. J.F. (Derick) Nixon, one of Canada's leading experts in the field of permafrost engineering, would add his expertise to this project from his home base in Calgary. Over the years, Derick had been actively involved in numerous projects for the National Research Council of Canada and was a member of the Canadian Geotechnical society.

I had the privilege of working with Derick throughout the eighties and early nineties on numerous laboratory frost heave and pipe uplift projects. He was intelligent, hard-nosed, mercurial, and temperamental, and demanded accurate, timely results from me. He would grill me if I showed the slightest amount of weakness or lack of confidence. At the same time, he didn't expect me to be simply a "yes" person. He wanted my input. He wanted to hear my opinions and ideas to evaluate them in his mind, even though he ended up dismissing most of them.

We had head bashing and clashes over the years, but somehow we both managed to survive. Although my slow, simple-minded nature did not match up to his quick-thinking intellectual mind, and his patience wore out frequently, somehow I could never pawn off these lab tests to anyone else. Derick always wanted me to be the guy (or perhaps the scapegoat) working for him. It was only in the latter years, just before he quit HBT Agra to become an independent consultant, that I finally discovered that the secret to getting on his good side was to pretend to have confidence and poise in everything I did and said—even if I didn't have the slightest clue what I was doing or talking about. After that, I got along with him just fine. It seems we always learn life's most valuable lessons at the tail end of things!

Initially, the drilling program was to start in late January or early February 1994. Since this was typically a slow time for work in Calgary, I had no problem taking time off to prepare for Russia. Conversely, this was a very busy time for Alex Costin, our logistics coordinator, as he worked tirelessly with Amiga and Heerema to sort out the details. Early on, he was the busiest person on the project.

The first thing we did as a group was to go downtown with Alex to a winter gear store to be outfitted with parkas and mukluks. It was going to be cold where we were going, and we wanted to be prepared for the elements. The mukluks we purchased weren't anything fancy, just made from the traditional cloth and rubber. They would keep our feet warm and dry. However, the parkas were extra fancy: Calberta Blizzard Gard goose down-filled coats extending below our hips. They were double zippered and had fox fur hoods. They would become especially useful on the cold nights at the weather station when the diesel heaters ran out of fuel and we lay shivering in our beds.

After our all-expenses-paid shopping spree was done, our next course of action was to complete first aid and arctic survival courses. This was done over a two-day period. St. Johns ambulance, recognized across Canada, gave us the first aid training in our company's auxiliary meeting room. Although we covered the basics, a special emphasis was placed on winter conditions and injuries that we might encounter, such as frostbite, hypothermia, accidents in and around the drilling rigs, basic cuts, and splints for broken bones.

The arctic survival course was delivered by Cottrell Survival Consultants. They showed us videos of survival techniques and emergencies pertaining to the Arctic, and once again, the focus was job related. A special emphasis was placed on situations in and around helicopters and cargo planes. We covered where the emergency beacons would be located, how to activate them in case they didn't automatically come on, starting a fire without firewood (since we would be in a treeless environment) using the aircraft's battery as a spark, and using aviation fuel for heating and cooking. We were also given a card showing the internationally recognized ground-air emergency codes, and shown how to use them.

We covered the basics of how to build different types of shelters to protect us from the elements, which in our case were the cold winter conditions. He showed us how to build quinzhees and snow caves, which are easier to build than igloos and take less time. Essentially, they are temporary shelters created by either shovelling snow into a large pile, then hollowing it out, or simply shovelling out a hole in the snow.

He covered dehydration and the importance of staying hydrated. Dehydration is often neglected when a person's focus in on staying warm. Always make sure you drink lots of water, especially when exerting energy.

Then we covered the basics of food. This included how and where to get food when the resources are limited and few animals are around, especially in barren landscapes with little or no vegetation. Penguins, he mentioned, are a good source of fat and energy, and people can live off them for months if necessary. We were taught how to capture them and ways to cook them. Their fat can also be used for fuel and making candles. (No, he didn't actually teach us about penguins because in the first place, penguins aren't found in the Arctic region, they only live in the Antarctic, near the South Pole. I was just checking to see if you were paying attention.)

As mentioned, throughout this preparation period, a lot of paper work needed to be filled out. This included SOS emergency cards, which are recognized worldwide and are used to cover costs for medical expenses, hospital stays, and medical air transportation and evacuations. Our home contact emergency numbers were also passed on to the company in the event of an accident.

Of course, our wills had to be made out, or made up to date. As I filled out these forms, I started to feel my comfort zone slipping away slightly. With all these "just in case" scenarios, I started wondering what I was getting myself into. I realized there were certain risks involved in this overseas excursion. I hoped everything would turn out okay.

Although I didn't have regrets or foreboding nightmares about the trip, I did have one vivid dream, a premonition of sorts, three weeks prior to our departure. In it, I was somewhere in Russia and I saw a fearsome, majestic image towering over me. It seemed to reach the clouds as the sun shone brightly upon it. It was a dazzling and magnificent sight, but at the same time, quite intimidating. Later, in Moscow, I was to encounter this vivid image from my dream.

Meanwhile, Alex Costin was busy preparing a traveller's list of things we needed for the project, including personal and toiletry items. Individually, we set about on our own, purchasing the many required and suggested items. I decided to convert my money to U.S. dollars, since they are more widely accepted around the world than Canadian money. It was also negotiated through Alex and Gazprom that the HBT Agra personnel would be paid in U.S. dollars.

By February 1, I had finished most of my list, and it was just a matter of waiting. "Hurry up and wait," would become the common mantra in the days ahead and throughout the trip. Occasionally, Alex dropped by to update me and the rest of the group on how things were developing. The Russians were in the process of assembling and organizing the drilling crews. Arrangements were being made through charter cargo and helicopter companies to move the drilling equipment to the site. The food situation and living quarters on the sites were also being arranged. Our travel arrangements and those of the Russians were being coordinated so that our overseas flight lined up with those of the drilling crews. On top of this, we needed good weather conditions for things to go smoothly. We couldn't travel to the sites if they were in the midst of a blizzard.

"Expect to leave by February 15," Alex said one day. He had come to the lab to update me. "Make sure you have everything that you need, and buy anything that you don't have already."

"I'll be ready," I assured him. I felt that I was as ready as I could possibly be, since I always liked to prepare thing well in advance and not be a last minute shopper.

As the date moved closer, Alex came again to tell me that weather conditions at the two sites were delaying things. They had encountered some huge snowfalls and air transportation to the sites would be difficult, if not impossible.

"We'll be delayed perhaps two more weeks. Be prepared to leave on, or about, the end of February."

At this point, I was still quite excited but anxious to get going. It was nervewracking, waiting. As a single person with no pets to take care of, I had no responsibilities to anyone. I had plenty of casual girlfriends, but none of the serious kind. I don't think they cared, one way or another, whether I went to Siberia or not. I don't even think they would miss me if I were sent to a Gulag camp, never to return.

"Larry who?"

Concerning my parents and two sisters, Marlene and Debbie, they were quite nonchalant and perhaps oblivious to my upcoming adventures. I had moved from Oliver, B.C. my hometown fourteen years previously, and only saw them once or twice a year anyways. Not that they didn't care or love me (at least that's what they told me whenever they phoned), but we tend to live in our own little worlds as adults.

Jim French, a friend of mine who was sharing the duplex I owned, would look after any unexpected issues at home.

The days went by quickly, and February stretched into March. Alex continued to update us every few days, as time was becoming critical. If it wasn't the weather creating havoc, it was the problem of obtaining charter cargo planes and helicopters due to conflicting schedules. It was becoming tedious, as we were anxious to get started. Winter would soon be turning to spring, and the work season in Calgary would start to get busy. My boss, Gary Wostradowski, wouldn't be enthused about losing me if this stretched into summer. Also, conditions at the sites on Baydaratskaya Bay were starting to deteriorate. With spring just around the corner, the ice was cracking, and breakups were underway with the thawing conditions. This was not good, as our program entailed moving the rigs onto the ice and drilling a few kilometers offshore. The situation was becoming a bit dicey.

Another possibility was that the project would be delayed until the following winter. This was the last thing we wanted to happen. Everybody was on edge. Alex and Jim Oswell, the engineer overseeing things from the Canadian perspective, were in daily consultations with the Heerema and Amiga personnel.

Once we knew that the project was a go, we would have to make the final arrangements for our flight overseas and hotel accommodations, and coordinate the pickup teams at the other end. Money in rubles or U.S. dollars would have to be advanced to us. At this point, we decided to go ahead with the required vaccination shots. There was no point in delaying that much longer. I don't know if there is a period for best efficacy, but we decided to go ahead anyways.

The four of us headed to downtown Calgary one afternoon to the travel clinic on 5th Avenue to get the DPT (diphtheria, polio, and tetanus), typhoid, and hepatitis A shots.

March turned into April. The poor conditions, including heavy snowfall at the weather stations, were starting to improve. The ten- to fifteen-foot snowdrifts were melting, then refreezing, allowing a hardening of the snow surface. This made conditions easier for the drilling rigs and personnel to move around, especially around the buildings. In my case, the biggest concern would be getting to the outhouse without being buried in the snow and needing a Saint Bernard to rescue me.

However, as the conditions on land got better, the ice conditions on the bay got worse. There were now open sections of water in the middle of the bay. Along the shoreline, the ice was still thick enough for the project to proceed, but for how long?

By mid-April, we were finally given our calls to action.

"Be prepared to leave on twenty-four hours' notice," Alex announced one day. "Make sure you go over your checklists. Take care of anything you need to do at home, get your bills paid and up to date, take care of any pets, whatever needs to be done."

I felt I was as prepared as I ever would be. I had most of my suitcases more or less packed with all the arctic gear stuffed into them. I had two large suit-cases containing my goose-down sleeping bag, huge parka, mukluks, lots of long johns, winter clothing, and two large carry-ons containing my toiletries, passport, list of emergency numbers, and credit cards. I put multiple copies of these important documents in my money belt. Since every ounce of weight was important, I went to the ludicrous extreme of even sawing my toothbrush in half to save an ounce or two.

Tuesday April 26, 1994

The words that I had been waiting to hear for three months finally came. "Larry, you guys are leaving tomorrow." Alex Costin said this as he made his rounds, visiting us and spreading the good news. After a brief chat about last minute details, he shook my hand.

"Good luck! I will give you your airline ticket and SOS card tomorrow. They are being fast tracked by courier and should be here before you leave in the afternoon. Bring your luggage, suitcases, documents, and everything you need for the project with you to work tomorrow. From work you will be taken by taxi to the airport."

He went upstairs to let Gary know that he was finally abducting me and I was no longer available to him for the next few weeks. Angela Binnie, my assistant, along with Gary, would take over the lab. Since it wasn't yet summer and work was slow, they would be able to handle it.

Alex had worked overtime on his duties to ensure all the details were looked after before we left. He had done a great job of making sure everything went smoothly for the project's initial preparations. Other than handing over our final documents the next day and a few odds and ends, his job was essentially done.

Jim Oswell would now oversee things from the Canadian perspective, although most of our direction would come from the Dutch engineering company Heerema and the Russian company Amiga.

Early Wednesday morning, I received an interoffice fax sent from Jim Oswell to Al Hanna and relayed to the observation team. Al was a senior engineer with HBT Agra, who would oversee things for Jim Oswell when he was out of office, or in Leiden, since he was splitting his time between the two. They would be our contact persons for personal situations arising back home, or for any project concerns we had.

Jim's message to Al said:

April 27, 1994

The latest word from Yamal with regards to the field program is this:

May 3rd. The drilling would start.

Ice roads around Yamal will remain open for one or two more weeks.

Ice road to Yamal is closed.

Fuel is available at Yamal and will be transported by helicopter to the site.

Weather is -5C, sunny, several meters of snow.

Lodging is primitive, but adequate. Reasonable food.

Hotel in Labytnangi is 50,000 rubles/night (US$30)

In Moscow, arrangements have been made to exchange US$800 to rubles.

The two Dutch observers will arrive in Moscow at 1400.

Hotel and accommodation and pickups have been arranged through the Heerema office including our arrival at Murmansk.

Good luck to Bob, Ray, John, and Larry.

This was it! It was now official, and the project was a go.

CHAPTER 3
CALGARY TO MOSCOW

Wednesday April 27, 1994
Day 1 (cont.)

Earlier this morning at work, Alex gave us our airline tickets and emergency SOS cards, then shook our hands and wished us good luck. (We had picked up our visas from him a few days earlier.) At this time he also gave us our final briefing. His secretary had arranged for the taxi company to pick us up with a van and take us to the airport. With all of our suitcases and carry-ons, we definitely needed a van compared to a normal sized taxicab.

At the Calgary Airport, going through the check-in counter at the departures level, it took a while to get everything tagged and checked in. Because we were in business class, they didn't charge us extra duties. In the lineup going through the x-ray machines, I proudly decided to take charge of our group. "Remember to pick up your belongings after you go through," I stated. Everyone ahead of me went through without any problems, but when I went through, the security alarm went off. I was taken off to one side and, like a criminal suspect, held my hands up while the security agent took out his security wand to check me thoroughly, from top to bottom, trying to locate my "terrorist weapon." It took him a while to hone in on it. The threat was the small metallic tin foil on my Tic Tacs container in my pant pocket. In his brilliant judgment, and after careful consideration, he decided to let me keep it. For the rest of the trip, I was to receive many extra personalized checks at airports because of that stupid container.

Ten minutes later, while sitting in the waiting lounge, I realized that the blue jacket I had been wearing up until the x-ray lineup was missing. I had forgotten it there. After reminding everyone not to forget their things, I ended up forgetting my jacket. I went back, picked it up, and quietly and sheepishly returned to my seat. Dolt! But John didn't seem to notice, Ray was too busy hunched over, writing little things in his diary, and Bob just grinned. I think I will lie low for a bit and let someone else take charge for a while.

Our flight itinerary is Calgary, Vancouver, Frankfurt, Moscow, Murmansk, Labytnangi, and finally the weather stations at Baydaratskaya Bay in northwest Russia. Our modes of transportation will be done through commercial airlines, cargo planes, and helicopters (and, if all else fails, probably dog sleds). Rather than going east through Toronto, we are taking a detoured route west so that our luggage goes direct, and we don't have to pick it up on the way. Our Canadian Airlines flight number 677 left on time at 3:30pm this afternoon and we just arrived here in Vancouver. I am waiting to board Lufthansa flight number 1072 to Frankfurt, West Germany scheduled to depart at 4:55pm.

— * —

So here I am back, reflecting upon everything that has happened so far, writing my diary in the waiting lounge of the Vancouver airport.

This first leg of the trip from Calgary to Vancouver has been very nice so far. I have never been in business class of a Boeing 737 before, or for that matter, on any other type of airline. They were even offering us free champagne as a celebration of what I thought was their merger with America Airlines, but I politely declined. I was too energetic and excited and wanted to stay focused. Oddly, I never heard any more about a merger between Canadian Airlines and American Airlines, but nevertheless, we were offered complimentary champagne.

It's amazing how, when I look back on this trip, either through the providence of God or by coincidences, I was able to experience the pinnacle of things at its finest, and the lowest of things at its worst. My trip starts off in business class on a first-class airline and, because of its coinciding (to the day) inaugural merger (or working agreement) with another airline, we were offered complimentary champagne. This is followed by transportation upon airlines and helicopters at the other end of the scale in a country noted for its dismal safety records. And then, later on, I was to go from living at a remote, primitive weather station, with an outhouse for a toilet and very basic food and amenities to, by a mistake from a driver, getting booked into a wrong hotel in Moscow and given an executive suite where, just one hour prior to my arrival, they had just refurnished the entire floor after months of renovations.

The mysteries of life!

— * —

In addition to the two large suitcases I have in cargo, I have two carry-ons next to me. They are bursting at the seams. Prior to take-off, a flight attendant came over and strapped them into the seat next to me. I'm glad I didn't have to pay extra for the seat. I thanked her. That is very wise on their part. You don't want luggage flying around if there is turbulence. The flight attendants do a great job and I admire them for that. After she gave safety procedures and seatbelt instructions in German over the P.A. system, our flight was on our way. Initially it seemed odd that here I am in Canada and the flight attendants are speaking German; but then I realized this is a German airliner.

The flight to Frankfurt aboard the Boeing 747 was relatively noneventful. Nonetheless, I did enjoy immensely the luxuries of flying business class. With the wide berth, the reclining seats were extra comfortable so one could stretch out, not like those cramped conditions found in economy class. In addition, how could I complain about all the personalized attention that the pretty German flight attendants gave us? I will enjoy this moment and not pity those poor peasants behind us, past the curtained doorway.

However, little was I to know that later on, I *would* become like one of those poor peasants, and have to endure sitting in the cramped conditions in the back of an Aeroflot cargo plane with cargo strewn about me. But that is futuristic, and I am getting ahead of myself. Enjoy the moment while I have it.

Including the complimentary drinks, the flight attendants handed out some very nice travel gift-packs that included such things as perfumes, miniature toothbrush, toothpaste, and razors.

Thursday April 28
Day 2

I enjoyed a very fine meal of Salmon Pastrami, veal, noodles, and strawberries before succumbing to the after effects for a snooze. My stomach was well satisfied. This was luxurious. I was starting to unwind after a stressful, but exciting, first day of adventures. Intrigue and adventure still awaits me though. Although I look forward with extreme anticipation, the work ahead will be a bit of a challenge.

After my snooze, I watched Free Willy on TV. The TV monitor displayed a map showing us our location along with GPS coordinates and outside temperature. When I checked it, it showed we were flying over the Shetland Islands at 990 km/hr, and with an outside temperature of -59C.

The -59C temperature surprised me. Cold, cold, cold! And yet, here we are, sitting in a nice cozy cabin, flying in the midst of this bitterly cold environment. As we approached Frankfurt and started our slow descent, we became immersed in heavy fog and cloud. With no visibility whatsoever, the pilots would obviously be flying on *Instrument Flight Rules* (IFR) and under the directions of the air traffic controller. With other unseen aircraft like us circling somewhere amongst the clouds, it was a bit unnerving, but, at the same time, a bit exciting. We were lost in the clouds and just hoping that modern technology and good communication skills between the pilot and airport traffic controllers were in play. We represented only a blip on their radar screens, but that blip meant a lot to me.

We landed safely at about noon Thursday April 28 (Frankfurt time, eight hours difference from Calgary time), but because of the delay in circling due to heavy traffic, our plane ended up half an hour late. We only had one hour to get to the other side of the terminal to catch Lufthansa flight 3210 to Moscow, but, by some huffing, puffing, and doing some running, we managed. With all the stress from the past few days, the memory of Frankfurt airport completely eludes me. Even the next day, I had no recollection of what the airport looked like. There were too many things going on to absorb everything and too many things ahead of us to think about.

We landed at Domodedovo Airport in Moscow three hours later, on time, at about 5:00pm Moscow time, accounting for a one-hour time difference.

We were scheduled to fly out at 11:30pm to Murmansk where we would stay a day or two, before moving on by cargo or chartered plane to Labytnangi. This is the closest town to our final destination, the remote weather stations at Baydaratskaya Bay. However, because of our delay in landing in Frankfurt, none of our luggage made it through. We found out through the *lost and found* that it was scheduled to arrive at 10:00pm. We thought nothing of this, since our flight left at 11:30pm and figured there wouldn't be any problems, so we carried on as planned.

We introduced ourselves to Sasha, a casually dressed young Russian from the Moscow Heerema office, whom we connected with by the traditional method of meeting someone in the airport you've never met before; with him holding a sign which read "Heerema." His job was to provide us with ground transportation to the Bykovo Airport, a domestic airport a few kilometers away. Two Dutch personnel, both with first names of Peter, were next to him. They will work with us on the drilling program as observers. Peter 1 and Peter 2 had met up with Sasha a few hours earlier. None of the Peters or the Canadians could speak Russian, and Sasha couldn't speak English, so we knew we would be in for an adventure over the next short while as we tried to communicate with each other. After a few awkward moments of introductions and hand gestures, we were shown to the van. From Jim Oswell's fax a few days ago, he didn't feel it necessary to book a hotel in Moscow for the few hours layover we had between flights, so Sasha proceeded to give us a tour of Moscow. Unlike his casual appearance, and his casual manners, when it came to driving there was nothing casual about that. With the pent up exuberance of a young man willing to show off his beloved city, and with seatbelts extra tight, for the next two hours we were given a whirlwind tour. I sat in the front seat next to Sasha as we flew around the city. I think I saw the Kremlin...perhaps a second or two of it. I saw brief glimpses of other magnificent historical buildings. Since I didn't do well in history class in high school, I haven't the faintest ideas what they were. But they did look impressive (whatever buildings they were). But the streets themselves, that was another story. Everything seemed rundown and dreary, lacking energy and vibrancy.

Impressions: First impressions were the uneven sidewalk and road conditions, I guess due to frost heave. There are many broken down cars along the road along with rusting cars. There is few service or gas stations. Drab conditions abound everywhere. Everything is in a state of decay. The buildings are color-less. Everything is just falling apart. Parks had trees and rough walkways, but nothing was landscaped. No flowers and few shrubs. A slew or a pond in the park here and there, and you see a number of people, families, and dogs there splashing around. Most buildings are large stone or concrete. Apartments are small and drab.

I see many (police officers?) standing at corners or in the streets. They are not intimidating, but rather the opposite. They seem to just be standing around and not really doing a whole lot. Street poles massively shifted and on the brink of toppling. Attitudes of people seem rather indifferent, no ambition (when working). The people however, when not working seem like all of us "westerners," happy, sad, indifferent, playful, the usual mix.

The gloomy conditions we saw on the streets were a reflection of what we also saw inside the airport, with its darkened interior, and its many unlit fixtures, both inside and outside the terminal. It seemed as if they wanted to save on their electricity bills. [In all fairness, this was still late winter with all the cheerless conditions I just mentioned. When spring finally did arrive, on the return trip, Moscow came alive and showed its true beauty and vibrant colors from the flowers, parks, and gardens that are abundant throughout the city. It truly is a majestic and beautiful city. It was just hibernating at this time.]

In between some self-conscious attempts to have a somewhat decent English/Russian conversation with Sasha, and with the shutter speed of my 35mm camera set to its fastest, I was able to snap a few pictures of the *what-chamacallit* impressive buildings as they whizzed by us.

About one hour into the tour, we came across a majestic sight which reawakened the memories of my dream I had a few weeks ago. As we slowed down to turn a corner, we approached a very steep hill that we proceeded to climb. Directly in front of us, stood the image of my dreams, a magnificent churchlike cathedral with a tall steeple in all its glorious splendor and gothic design. From the steep, uphill angle we were on, it seemed to disappear into the clouds and heavens. With the setting of the sun, a halo of brilliant orange rays was splayed upon the clouds behind it, creating the illusion of burning clouds and making for an awe-inspiring spectacle. I knew instantly that this was the image I had seen in my dreams. I snapped a picture of it the moment I saw it. I then pointed to it and asked, "Chto eto (what is it)?" to Sasha.

Either Sasha was too busy keeping at least three of the four wheels on the road, or he didn't hear or understand me, so I didn't find out until much later what the image was. On the internet, after comparing images to my photograph, I found out this was not a church and steeple at all, but rather a hotel. Built in the 1950s and originally named *Hotel Ukraine*, it has since been renovated and renamed *Radisson Royal Hotel*. Standing on the western banks of the Moscow River, it stands thirty stories high and has one thousand guest rooms. It is a mixture of "Stalinist architecture and renaissance finery."]*

*[www.moscow-hotels.net/Ukraine-hotel//]

Our tour ended shortly after this and we were driven to the Novotel hotel where we could rest up and quench our thirst with a beer or two in the lounge area. Sasha indicated that he would pick us up later to take us to Bykovo Airport.

Two young ladies, one at a piano and one with a flute, played melancholy songs in the relaxed ambiance of the lounge area. We chatted with Peter 1 and Peter 2 and got better acquainted with them. They are both in their mid-twenties, single, and are the typical energetic males their age, looking for adventure. They gladly accepted this job offer when Heerema offered them a contract. They, alongside Ray Hunt and John Fitcher, will be the drilling observers, while I will be the laboratory observer. Bob Forsythe would oversee everything and report back to Leiden and Calgary. As the soft tunes played on and the beers were quietly consumed, the adrenalin rush from the past twenty-four hours was starting to wear off, and I was getting tired. I was sure everybody else in the group felt the same way as I did.

Sasha eventually came back with the van and drove us to Domodedovo International Airport. A tough lady agent, both emotionally and physically, representing Lufthansa Airlines argued with, and physically fought a Russian cart handler to hand over some carts and trolleys for our luggage, as we stood there in appreciative amusement. Later on in Moscow, on my return trip, I was to get involved in another heated discussion for a cart, which led to the appearance of a tall stranger to assist me; a person who perhaps was an angel in disguise. After picking up our "delayed luggage" at the luggage carousel from the 10:00pm flight from Frankfurt, we crammed everything into the van, and Sasha drove us to Bykovo Airport, a domestic airport. We arrived at around 11:00pm. At the check-in there, we were given the bad news. There was not enough time to check everything in for the 11:30pm flight. Bob pleaded, whined, did everything in his powers, but to no avail. Even though our luggage was all labeled "priority," the lady at the ticket counter would not budge. It was too late to catch the flight to Murmansk. After "Big Bob" lost his dueling match of wits with her, she eventually rebooked us for the next day's 10:00am flight. The airline provided us with complimentary accommodations at the Novotel hotel and also sent a small bus, specifically for us, to take us there. As we sat scattered about in various seats on the dark, unlit bus, I took a moment to snap a picture of Bob. There he was, sitting at the back of the bus in a striped referee's shirt, arms folded, luggage strewn all over the floor and seats, with this big grin on his face. Nothing seemed to perturb him. Classic Bob, and a classic Kodak moment!

We arrived at the Novotel hotel about 12:30 in the morning. It is a four or five star western style hotel in the sense that English is widely spoken and many foreign business people and companies stay there. My roommate this night and throughout most of the trip was Ray. I was sure that he, like me, was absolutely exhausted and ready to crash. Lights out, I slept well, until the dreaded jet-lag hit me. But Ray, who is about twenty years older than me, had other thoughts and more energy than I did. He snuck out of the room, rounded up Bob and John, and headed to the stripper club downstairs where, once again, their taste buds were quenched along with some eye-candy. Their entertainment, however, was cut short when the lady, who also doubled as an escort, had some other business to take care of and had to leave early. The next morning at breakfast, Ray told me about their escapades. He knew because of my conservative nature that I probably wouldn't have attended anyways, and thus, didn't ask me.

CHAPTER 4
MURMANSK

Friday April 29
Day 3

We had a very nice buffet-style breakfast in Novotel's main restaurant this morning and chatted briefly with some businessmen who are working in Russia as well. Earlier this morning, Bob let the Heerema office and Jim Oswell, know about our delays and layover, which affected our previous bookings of the hotel in Murmansk. It also affected our continuing flight from Murmansk to Labytnangi. Everything was now delayed or on hold.

Sasha came at 8:30 to take us to the domestic Bykovo Airport. There, despite another long delay in having our luggage weighed, and paying extra duties, everything went smoothly. We boarded the three-engine Tupolev Tu54, a workhorse of the Aeroflot Airlines. I just hoped this horse wasn't too tuckered out while we flew on it.

At this point we gave our thanks and final goodbyes to Sasha, who did well, driving us around Moscow and taking us to the two Moscow airports. I gave another silent thanks to God that we were still in one piece. Sasha was to pick me up a few weeks later, on my return flight home where he handed me that ominous telefax, "URGENT! DO NOT LEAVE MOSCOW!" from the head office of Heerema.

We took off, on time, leaving our adventures of Moscow behind us and looked forward with excitement and a bit of trepidation to the new adventures which lay ahead.

PS We are taking off. We're in the air despite a loud whine in the engines.

It reminds me of the story which might have been my sister Marlene, and her husband Ray Tolman, when they were on a flight to Mexico. After reaching cruising altitude they heard a sudden bang, and, after looking out the window, noticed one of the engines on fire. Horrified, they didn't know what to do.

But the pilot came on over the intercom. "Ladies and gentlemen, we would just like to inform you that one of our engines just caught fire. But don't worry, we have put it out. We still have three good engines, but will be about ten minutes late on arriving at our destination.

"Whew," Marlene and Ray sighed in unison.

A few minutes later, another bang was heard as another engine caught fire. Again, Marlene and Ray looked out the window in horror. Again the pilot came on the intercom, and reassured everyone that the fire would be dealt with. He also took the time to explain that the plane was quite capable of flying with two engines, but that the flight would now be delayed half an hour.

"Whew," Marlene and Ray sighed in unison again.

But a few minutes later another bang was heard as a third engine caught fire. Again the pilot came on, confidently reassuring everyone that the plane could still fly on one engine, but that now the delay would be one hour.

At this point, Marlene, in exasperation, turns to Ray and says, "Man, I hope we don't lose another engine. Otherwise, we'll be up here all day!"

I wish life were like that as I continued to listen to our bumblebee drone on. After a slightly turbulent but non-eventful flight, I still counted the engines to make sure they were all there when we landed in Murmansk. But I counted only three. Oh, oh, but then I remembered; this is a *three*-engine plane. "Whew," I sighed, only to myself.

— * —

We made it safely to Murmansk. It was cool, with a small amount of snow on the ground, and temperature of +10C. This was light jacket weather, where Moscow was more T-shirt weather with temperatures around +15C. The airport in Murmansk was very plain and nothing more than a shack.

The only thing that stands out in my mind about the airport is that stupid screen door at the main entrance. As we sat in the lounge area, waiting for our pickup, that screen door would constantly "screech" and "bang" shut every time someone walked through it (which was always). All someone had to do was take the initiative and put small, soft cushion or rubber pads on the corners and oil its hinges, and silence would be bliss. Instead, we had to put up with the constant banging. We only had to put up with this for half hour or so, but I wonder how the workers there managed, working in that atmosphere all day. Sadly, I think it reflects upon, and shows the general apathy the Russian people have. Rather than taking the initiative, without someone having to tell them what to do, and doing it with their own free will, they probably felt it wasn't their responsibility. Or perhaps they didn't want to step out of line. Their lives have been so rigorously controlled throughout their history that habits of conformity and acceptance are hard to break. So, if I ever go back to Russia and happen to fly into Murmansk, the first thing I'm going to do is check to see if that stupid screen door has been fixed or replaced. To be on the safe side, I'll bring some bumper pads and a can of WD-40.

Nadisha and her two assistants from Amiga, a company representing Gazprom, met us at the airport and we took the local main bus back to Murmansk, forty minutes away. The bus was old, decrepit, and very hot. I guess the driver couldn't control the heat. Along the bumpy road, we saw many cars broken down, comparable to that in Moscow. We are staying at the Arktika hotel at US$104 per night.

[In 2009, this hotel was renovated and reopened in 2014 as the Azimut Hotel Murmansk. At sixteen stories in height, it is classified as the tallest building, not only in Murmansk, but also, inside the Arctic Circle.]

Murmansk is located in northwest Russia at the end of a deep bay of the Barents Sea. Because of the Gulf Stream and the North Atlantic Current, it is an ice-free port and a very important hub for shipping and fishing to Europe and the Arctic. It lies at 69 degrees north latitude. The population of the city is about 450,000. It has numerous skyscrapers, one after the other, alongside the hills. I think there is more color and seems richer than Moscow.

Early this afternoon, Ray and I decided to go for a walk. It was raining and overcast, but refreshing. As we walked along the somewhat deserted, wet sandy road, skirting the occasional puddle of water from the spring thaw, we were drawn to the sound of loud "booms" off in the distance. Every few seconds, at regular intervals, these booms reverberated off the high-rise buildings towards us. Our curiosity was aroused. We had to put our Sherlock Holmes caps on and investigate.

As we meandered along, I noticed out of the corner of my eye, a young lad perhaps nine or ten years old, following us a short distance away. He seemed shy, yet curious.

We continued on. Maybe I'm just a suspicious person (but then again, maybe I have seen too many James Bond movies and read too many Andy McNab SAS stories), but I decided to keep a wary eye on him just the same, as he followed us, keeping his distance. He somehow seemed to know we were foreigners.

It is interesting how people, perhaps especially in other countries and especially children, know immediately when someone is out of place and not a local. I didn't think we looked *that* out of place. Our outerwear seemed normal, typical, like everyone here. They didn't have large labels on the back saying, "Humans inside these coats are made in Canada." Must be the way we walk or carry ourselves. Maybe Ray's white beard gave us away.

A few minutes later, we entered the construction site that was causing the noise. There was no safety fence like those typically found at North American sites.

A tall rig with an impact hammer, smoke pumping out, was pounding reinforced concrete (precast) piles into the semi-frozen ground, laying the groundwork for a new high-rise building. Every few seconds, the weighted hammer would drop onto these vertical piles, driving them to their appropriate depth. Thirty or forty piles, almost haphazardly, were sticking out from the ground ranging in height from about five to eight feet.

Heat from buildings thaws frozen ground, or permafrost, and causes uneven settling. To prevent this, a typical foundation design might include a rigid insulation pad laid on the ground, followed by an eighteen-inch layer of gravel. This layer needs to be thick enough so that the permafrost table moves up into the pad and the annual active frost zone (active layer) will therefore occur in the fill (gravel) where the freeze-thaw effects are negligible. The concrete foundation, connected to the piles in some form or another (or perhaps resting on them, I'm not sure), would sit three feet above this gravel layer, allowing an air gap between the ground and it. This prevents heat from thawing the ground. (That's enough engineering lessons for the day from my limited knowledge of permafrost and foundation design. No tests will be given.)

By this time, the young boy had caught up to us, and after developing enough courage, tried his limited English on us. For a small fee, he wanted to be our guide. At least that's what he told us.

I think if we asked him where a restaurant was, he would probably have taken us home, told his mom to play along, and present us with the words, "The best restaurant in town." And, he could have gotten away with it too as most restaurants and stores have little or no signage anyways depicting their services. And, I suppose there are a lot of small mom and pop stores, restaurants, and places here in Murmansk. In this case, it could be listed as a mom and son restaurant. With mom doling out the food, and our bellies happily content, all would be well in the world. On top of that, mother and son team would be a few dollars richer with the restaurant fees and guide commission. Also, mom would be very proud of her son, with his entrepreneurial spirit as well.

Either that, or he was a small Russian Mafioso "in training" doing some spying on us. Maybe he was willing to offer us his "protection services" in this "very dangerous town" for a small fee.

There were a few times on this trip that we had a lad or two, come over wanting to be our "guide(s)." I think it was part curiosity, part attempting their primitive English skills, and also perhaps trying to make a bit of money. We found them charming and not too persistent, unlike the Gypsies commonly found in the larger cities.

But he was friendly, nice, and polite; and so were we, in the sense that we didn't tell him to "buzz off." We politely said we weren't interested...although our stomachs disagreed vehemently. We were hungry and would soon need a place to eat.

We told our stomachs to be quiet as we headed back to the hotel, the lad now straggling far behind us, kicking up a rock here and there, or tossing a pebble into the pools of water; typical of what boys do when they are bored. But it was good for him to at least try.

After exchanging money at 1,830 rubles per USD, and checking in, Nedella [Nadisha] came back and, along with her companion Alexander, we went touring, with her being the tour guide. After buying small Russian dolls, we went for supper. Café after café was closed until finally we found a very good one about six blocks up, and three blocks left, from the hotel. She was upset and a bit saddened, so I tried to cheer her up. I think overall, though, she enjoyed herself. I had a great time. Our bus picks us up at the hotel at 7:30am. Charter leaves at 9:00am. Goodnight.

I found Nadisha to be a very charming person. Very short in stature, pleasant features, she displayed a gentle, determined spirit as she led us along the almost deserted streets in search of a restaurant. She spoke fairly good English so I was able to converse with her a little. She was saddened because she was trying to impress us and show off the city she loved, and yet, everything was closed. Eventually we found a restaurant and had a pleasant meal. I expressed my gratitude for her efforts and she seemed comforted by that. She is a very fine lady.

CHAPTER 5
REROUTED TO NADYM

Saturday April 30
Day 4

This morning at 7:30, we boarded a bus that took us from the hotel to the airport. We got there at 8:30 expecting to charter out at 9:00, then waited in the lounge until 10:30. We boarded a small, twin-engine prop cargo plane from the rear. All our luggage and supplies were stashed in the middle, with us sitting on plain benches on each side. No seat belts, just simple straps to hold us in. We flew for a few hours expecting to land in Labytnangi, but ended up landing in Nadym.

We are in Nadym. Anyways, back to our landing. We needed all hands on the cargo as it sat in the middle of the plane, loosely tied. We had to keep an eye on it as we landed or took off so that there wasn't any sudden shift. This was a charter flight specifically for the project. There were the six of us alongside about eight or ten Russian drillers and workers. None could speak English, but, with a bit of sign language and translation books, we managed. The flight was quite noisy. The Russians sliced up a fish and gave a slice to all of us (probably smoked or dried cod), and warm beer which we all shared.

This was our first introduction to the Russian drilling crew that we will be working alongside. A few more were to arrive at the site later. They were all well behaved, clean-shaven, dressed in casual flannel shirts, sweaters, and medium-weight jackets. Because of the noisy conditions, no one really spoke too much other than the usual greetings. By sharing their meagre meal with us, the Russians continued the age-old custom, and somewhat religious tradition, of breaking bread and drinking wine with the weary traveller who shows up at your doorstep; except in this case, they were breaking a fish and drinking warm beer with us in the back of a cramped, equipment-laden cargo plane.

We were supposed to fly to Labytnangi, then stay for a day or so, but we landed here in Nadym, and then found out we were stranded due to bad weather in Labytnangi (our adventures continue one after the other). We got bused to the local hotel here, and apparently are staying for three nights, since, probably due to the May Day holiday, can't go anywhere. The hotel here is quite bad, actually probably the worst I've ever been to in my life. But mind you, I have also experienced the best in the world as well. 50,000 rubles (US$28) I believe, a night. I shared with Ray Hunt again. The rooms are actually adequate. There is a shared bathroom per floor. No toilet paper (but we brought our own). We came prepared.

When I walked into Hotel Polynara and saw its outdated "flowery" wallpaper with its pealing and curled edges trying, in a futile attempt, to cheer up an otherwise dismal place, I had a déjà vu feeling come over me. Somewhere I had experienced or seen this before. Immediately I thought about my grandfather Clem and his family, on my dad's side, and about his Russian ancestry. The classic style of the antiquated furniture from a bygone era, the wallpaper, the ambiance of the room, all seemed to fit in, and be a part of their world. I could visualize the world he lived in and the hardships they encountered as they tried to eke out a living, plowing fields with oxen and raising livestock.

Many of us, for whatever reason, have had the "been there before" feelings, and I have had them on more than one occasion. But here is my theory on Déjà vu. Through our genes and DNA, we inherit a lot of talents, skills, and abilities from our ancestors such as music, art, athleticism, farming, and so on. But do we not also perhaps, inherit some of the sights, sounds, smells, thoughts, that they, our ancestors experienced, as they developed their music, art, athleticism, farming, etc. If, for example, our ancestors came from Russia (as mine did), and were farmers, and we inherited a farming talent through our DNA and genes, would we not also have déjà vu experiences of some of the sights, sounds, smells, thoughts that they had as they farmed the lands back in Russia?

— * —

We went for a bite to eat, but the cafes are very small and dumpy (as in Murmansk). But interestingly, we walked and walked, and everywhere we went, they were closed for one reason or another. A Russian from upstairs, who spoke English, showed us where there were a couple. The one we found open, though, was first-class, same as last night. The waitress didn't know English, but we were able to get a good meal of cucumber and tomato salad, a second salad which consisted of perhaps pickled onions, mushrooms, a small fish, eggs and whatever, perhaps chicken. We don't know all that was in it, but it was actually quite good. Along with juice, beer, and coffee, it came out to about 68,000 rubles for the six of us, approximately US$38.

Over the next few nights, other than one time in which they were closed, we ate our suppers here at this *Restaurant 65* as it was called. This was probably named in connection to being located on the 65th parallel. The Arctic Circle starts at the 66th latitude. The waitress, Eva, was also the owner of the place and served us wonderful meals and was very accommodating to us. Of course we couldn't really communicate what we wanted other than, "We are hungry boys, feed us please." Actually, for that matter, she didn't even have menus, perhaps typical of most small restaurants here. The menus were simply given by word of mouth. But all the meals we eventually had here were all very good, and she served us with warmth and kindness. The 30-minute walk here and back each night was well worth it.

All the buildings are monotone, drab concrete monsters. The playground areas are very small, although we did see a really nice one. It's almost like a modern slum area. The souvenir stands and stores, as in Murmansk, are very sparse. The six of us played rummy (crazy rummy) until about 12:30am. I won easily. Sunset is around 10:00pm each day. Interestingly, you see many people going for walks; moms, dads, kids (not many teenagers). There are very few cars. Must now make some water and purify it with drinking tablets. It looks like tomorrow we sit tight. We need to talk to our Calgary office or Heerema office in Leiden, but the telephone system is very poor, and is difficult to connect internationally. But Bob expects a call tomorrow, via Satellite, to update us as to whether to sit tight or not. So far, it has been many interesting challenges and, I would say, a total blast to experience the different cultures of the world. Bye.

The image I saw in my dream three weeks before going to Russia.

Bob Forsythe (center), and Peter 1 and Peter 2 in the bus in Moscow.

In Murmansk. (l-r), Alexander, Ray Hunt, Nadisha, John Fitcher, and Bob Forsythe.

Five of the six member observation team in front of Arktika hotel, Murmansk.
(l-r), Peter 2, Peter 1, John Fitcher, Larry Ritco, and Bob Forsythe.

Bob Forsythe, the observation team leader, and John Fitcher, Canadian drilling observer.

Ray Hunt, Canadian drilling observer.

The cargo plane at Nadym airport after we were rerouted
there due to bad weather in Labytnangi.

Backside of the cargo plane with Ray Hunt (left) looking on.

Birds-eye view of the terrain we flew over.

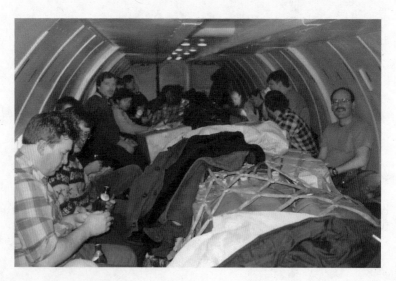

The author (right) amongst the Russian drillers in the cargo plane.

Nadym.

Nadym with John, Bob, and the two Peters to the right.

May Day festivities in downtown Nadym.

Pastry delights at the bazaar in Nadym.

Lela, our interpreter (center), and Bob.

Following the tracks of a baby stroller to
where the action was in downtown Nadym.

Bob using the satellite phone to update everyone in Leiden,
Holland while John Fitcher looks on.

Ray Hunt writing little things down in his diary at the hotel Polynara, Nadym.

The author standing beside a reindeer sled just outside Restaurant 65, Nadym.

A poster I saw of four beautiful ladies in their fur coats and
Shapka Ushanka hats advertising some sort of festival.

Labytnangi.

Enjoying our first meal in Labytnangi at the hotel.
(l-r), Bob, Ray, Peter 2, John, and Peter 1.

Arthur, our interpreter.

Safety meeting with Arthur (center left) at the hotel in Labynangi, relaying information to us about the site conditions.

CHAPTER 6
MAY DAY CELEBRATIONS

Sunday May 1
Day 5

This morning I was preparing my usual breakfast of a granola bar, Nutribar, and brown iodine-laced drinking water, when there was a knock on the bedroom door. Expecting to see Bob, I went to answer it. Bob had changed dramatically since I last saw him. Instead of his 6' 10" 265-pound frame greeting me, there was a small, beautiful brunette, barely 5'2" tall, standing there. Delicately built, she had tender dark brown eyes. She wore a black fur coat and had a matching fur *shapka ushanka* adorning her head. Her long, slender fingers were kept warm by black leather gloves. I could tell her fingers were long and slender because she had her gloves off, holding them in one hand. She wore black, semi high-heeled boots to keep her tiny feet cozy during the cold winter months. Not that I really noticed her. She accepted my long gaze with nonchalance. She was with another person, but it took me a while to really notice him there. Some of my preconceived images of Russia were true after all, and I realized that perhaps I had made a good decision to come and work on this project.

"I am Lela, the interpreter. This," as she gestured towards the man next to her, "is Alexander Zubov." By this time, Ray, upon hearing a woman's voice, was now at the door beside me, gaping at the sight beholding him.

Alexander, through Lela, then introduced himself to us as the *consul general* of Gazprom, a direct representative of the government, and welcomed us to

Nadym. As Lela continued to interpret, and our eyes and attention focused on her, I didn't catch too much of what she said in describing Alexander's duties. She was either a poor interpreter, or the small possibility that our minds were elsewhere. Probably the latter. When I finally did notice Alexander, I realized that, with his expensive suit and tie along with his official title as *consular general*, he required our polite, dutiful attention and respect when in his presence. After their brief and distinguished introductions, they went next door to acquaint themselves with everyone else.

Now fully awake, I looked at Ray to see what he had to say. Underneath his reddish beard and English accent he muttered something which I could neither understand, nor interpret. (Perhaps if I got Lela back in here, she could interpret for me, English to English.) He then sat down on his bed and proceeded to jot little things down in his diary. At this point I thought, "This just might turn out to be a great day." Little was I to know, we would be in for some unexpected dangers that night, watching our backs, as the May Day celebrations rocked on, all over Russia.

— * —

Later that afternoon, Lela was back, without Alexander. There was a bazaar and a flea market in town, and she asked if we would be interested in a tour. *As if*, we were going to decline. Of course, without hesitation, we took her up on her offer. After retrieving our coats and cameras, and Lela and Bob leading the way, the rest of us tagged along like a gaggle of goslings following mother and father goose, trying not to get lost amongst the crowd, or left behind, as we stopped occasionally to take a picture of two.

During our walk, we saw block after block of the same grey, lookalike concrete apartments, mostly eight to ten stories high. With the semi-frozen, sandy landscape in front of us, it seemed as if the city was built upon an ancient, flat seabed. There were few concrete sidewalks, and mostly natural, compacted sand made the roads. There was no vegetation or trees whatsoever, because, either the city was newly built, or the environment didn't support it.

A constant trickle of people in various garb and ages walked amongst us, some pulling baby strollers with babies happily tucked away under warm blankets or big fluffy jackets, while others were out shopping with shopping bags full of items in preparation for the weekend festivities. We followed the imprints in the sand of a set of stroller wheels as they led us to the heart of the downtown market. The city of about seventy thousand was in a festive mood. Colorful kiosks and tables were set up with people selling baked goods, pastries, homemade soups, and gourmet dishes. I wasn't sure if this market was every weekend, or just this May Day holiday, but either way, we had fun exploring and taking pictures. Although the displays looked tempting, no one in our group bought anything, since we would be eating soon at Eva's restaurant. We were also told that some of the products, especially agricultural, still had high levels of radiation from the fallout of Chernobyl in the spring of 1986, and from the Bara and Barents seas, the dumping grounds for nuclear radioactive wastes. Unfortunately, for the people who lived here, they couldn't be choosy. They had no choice. This just added to their already harsh lives as they tried to eke out a living here.

After we finished our explorations and picture taking, Lela and Bob led the group back to the hotel. After a couple hours rest and relaxation, we once again made the trek along the sandy road to Eva's restaurant. When we arrived at *Restaurant 65*, the night was still young, but the place was filling fast.

May Day, also known as "Spring and Labor Day," is a time when the Russian people spend time with family and friends in celebration of springtime, gardening, and flowers. This day lost its Socialist meaning after the Soviet Union's collapse. For one hundred years, from 1890 to 1990, May 1ˢᵗ was a symbol of class struggle in Russia with workers demanding better working conditions and higher wages. Workers held annual protests on this day from 1890-1917. On May 1, 1918, this day became a public holiday known as, "The Day of International Solidarity of Workers." Most cities and towns held parades and marches on this day until 1990. In 1992, the Russian parliament renamed this holiday as "Spring and Labor Day."

(Summarized from; www.timeanddate.com/holidays/russia/spring-and-labor-day).

We waited for Eva at the entrance, who, upon recognizing us, graciously welcomed us to one of the few tables left. As we sat down, she listed off the evening's meal, all of course spoken in her native tongue.

"Spasibo," was our lone, thankful response. Our Russian was improving. We didn't need translation books for that one, but at the same time, still had them in our pockets.

The atmosphere was friendly and lively with a hub of conversations throughout the room. Everybody was moderately enjoying their drinks and eating their meals. A few people from other tables, recognizing us as foreigners, greeted us jovially. We settled in nicely amongst the crowd, but somehow, we were mistakenly labelled, initially in a friendly manner, as "Americans." We tried to explain to them that we were "Kanadtsy," Canadian, and not Americans, but nobody seemed to understand. A band was setting up on stage, off to one side, gearing up for the evening's festivities.

Twenty minutes in, after our initial drinks were served, a waitress, other than Eva, came and presented us with platters of food; wiener schnitzels, three types of salads including the usual cucumber and tomato, salted or pickled fish entrees, and a sufficient number (at least for the time being) of beers and vodkas. It was a night of celebrations to look forward to. Good food, good people, good conversations, what more could a person ask for. After we ate our meals, and the plates taken away, the evening turned into a night of music, dancing, drinking, and toasts.

The band started playing and their lead singer started the night off with an energetic, lively Russian ballad. Toasts were cheerfully given from one table to another as the singer, in his husky baritone voice, dedicated the first song, incorrectly, to us, "The Americans."

At about this time, as more people continued to flow into this Restaurant-turned- nightclub, three young, attractive ladies walked in, looking for a place to sit. Since we probably had the only seats yet available, they came over and presumptuously, but politely, sat down, next to us. We felt flattered and honored to have them sit with us, but at the same time felt awkward with the language barrier between us. But Bob took charge quickly and after finding out their preferences, ordered drinks for them. Meanwhile, the rest of us quietly got our Russian translation books out and by furtively glancing down at them now and then, hoping not to look like dorks in the process, tried to provide them with some sort of decent conversation.

However, this did not sit well with the people at the table next to us, especially one man in particular, who seemed to have an animosity to "Americans" hitting on their women. Initially his catcalls and banter were friendly in nature, and we took it all in stride. The party continued on.

When supper duties were finished, Eva came over to visit with Bob. Soon afterwards, she and Bob proceeded to the dance floor to dance the night away. Despite his big frame, Bob was a pretty good dancer. And with his charming, boyish grin, I'm sure women were constantly falling for him. The three ladies at our table were soon escorted to the dance floor as well, by the two Peters, and John Fitcher, while Ray and I sat quietly, enjoying the atmosphere, sipping our beer and vodka.

The night wore on, more drinks were consumed, and the verbal and non-verbal skills improved, slowly breaking down the cultural barriers. This all added to the irritation of our Russian friend next to us as he became more belligerent. He was a small, yet fiery person, who wouldn't quit. His taunts become more aggressive and his voice got louder over the music. At this time, we didn't need our dictionaries to tell us what he was saying, other than "Go home you Americans," along with a few expletives.

He continued on with his tirade for a while, and then said something which drew a swift response from everyone around him. The atmosphere at that moment changed. The room suddenly grew quieter. We never did find out what he said, but the people around him weren't happy. He went over the line, and everyone told him, in no uncertain terms, to cool it. Even the ladies, including the waitress and Eva, came over to tell him to knock it off. We tried to stay cool and keep quiet, but now knew the situation was starting to boil over.

What happened next, to this day, I'm still not sure if I heard or saw the events correctly. When he made those last disparaging remarks to us, the conversations in the room became quieter. Other than the band continuing to play and the singer singing, the attention now focused on us. Up to this point, other than the words "You Americans," everything was spoken in the Russian language. Perhaps, in one last attempt to intimidate us and save face, he stood up. He wasn't very tall, and his words were tougher than his build.

Pointing to himself and with a loud voice, and in perfect English, he declared, "I'm with the Russian mafia."

Nobody spoke, as everybody was trying to collect his or her thoughts. Even the continuous vodka toasting came to a brief halt, as the focus was on what happened next.

But Big Bob Forsythe, our leader, didn't need long to collect his thoughts, or wits for that matter. They were collected. He took on the challenge. He stood up, all 6"10" of himself, faced his opponent, grinned, and pointing to himself said, "I'm with the mafia too!"

Why he made that statement, I'll never know. I never did ask him. Perhaps he had a few too many drinks and was sick and tired of the rantings, and at that point couldn't care less what he said, or perhaps he spoke those words to spite his opponent. I was going to ask Ray the next day if he heard and saw the same things that I heard and saw, but I forgot. I still wonder today what their recollections are, of what took place that night at Restaurant 65.

At this point, the Russian had no comeback. He meekly walked over to our table and faced Bob. With Bob towering over him, and the little guy straining his neck to look "way up," he extended his hand in friendship and respect. Bob shook his hand. The Russian then quietly headed back to his table where he spent the rest of the evening in relative silence. He had no more taunts directed our way. The party continued on, vodkas were replenished, the dancing continued, the band played on into the night, and the May Day, or should I say "The Spring and Labor Day" celebrations, continued on in the traditional way that the Russians celebrated. World War 3 between the Russians and us "Americans" was averted by Bob. That was the end of the hostilities. Or so we thought.

Later on, during the evening, Ray had to go to the bathroom. He leaned over to me and said, "Larry, I have to go to the bathroom." At first I didn't understand why he was telling me this. Perhaps he wanted to check if I had to pee. I didn't.

I replied, in a state of stupor, "That's nice."

He leaned over closer, looked me straight in the eye and repeated, more urgently this time, "Larry, I have to go to the bathroom!"

I gazed at him a bit longer. The few too many vodkas still had control of me, and I still didn't know "what the heck" Ray was onto. Then it finally dawned on me, and I realized what he was trying to say.

"Oh, okay, right. Yeah, let's go."

We were in foreign territory and some of the Russians, who had a few too many drinks, probably didn't exactly approve of us, especially considering us as "Americans" hitting on their ladies. Heading alone into a washroom, with a bunch of Russian drunks following you, is not a guarantee for a safe pee. I escorted Ray to the washroom and stood patiently outside his stall, abiding my time, trying hard not to look stupid.

As I stood there patiently holding up the wall, I thought to myself, "Well, this is all good for Ray, he is safely inside his stall, but what about *me*? Standing there alone, how was *he* going to help *me* if I was attacked?" But, there were no conflicts. Ray had a safe pee, and we both came back to the table, with no black eyes or sore guts.

In the wee hours of the morning, we were tuckered out from the dancing and our primitive Russian language lessons we were trying out on our newly found lady friends, so we took the thirty minute walk back to the hotel. It was semi-dark as the sun wasn't yet quite on call for its twenty-four hour a day duty. Our normal, leisurely pace was quickened this evening as three or four drunks followed us from the bar, slowly weaving behind us, yelling and swearing at "us Americans." We prudently didn't respond, nor look back. We kept walking straight ahead and eventually they lost interest in us.

But unfortunately for us, we didn't all make it back to the hotel that night. Only five made it back. We lost Peter 1. Not that we were all lousy at arithmetic and couldn't count, or through negligence on our part, we forgot that we had six to start with and only five returned; it was probably due to the simple fact that we just didn't care (not to mention that we had too much to drink). I wondered what the war room back home would think. Only five days in and already, we were down a man for the project.

But it wasn't that Peter was beat up, lying in a sewer gutter in some back alley, a casualty of the drunk men following us; nor had he fallen victim to the short man of questionable mafia status. Instead, he was a casualty to a young, pretty female. And no, she wasn't a honeypot, a trap set to lure him for his passport, or his wealth, or the vast secrets he held pertaining to this project. He succumbed to that irresistible thing called "love."

After chatting it up with one of the ladies sitting next to us at our table, he stayed behind and didn't come back until much later that morning. It's amazing how love transcends all language barriers.

The next night, Peter was out again with the same lady. We didn't enquire about his romantic escapades, but later in the day, he told us about this new "friendship." She took him home to meet her parents and family, and they had a simple, pleasant evening.

During our preparation phase, before coming to Russia, Alex Costin, our logistics coordinator, warned us to stay away from the Russian ladies as, at times, they are *setups*. They work in partnerships with others and engage in things ranging from petty thefts and stealing of passports, to more sinister criminal activities, especially when the mafia is involved.

But the ladies whom we met and sat with, at the restaurant that night, were innocent enough. They simply wanted to spend the weekend in celebration of the May Day long holiday and have a good time with their fellow Russian comrades and visitor guests. I think, in the end, they, along with the rest of us, ended up having just that...a very good time.

Back at the safety of the hotel, it was too early to sleep, so we stayed up and played crazy rummy until 4:30 in the morning. We placed a heavy three-pound loaf of Russian Black Bread and a case of beer on Peter 1's chair where he normally sat, in memory of him, as we played with only five people now. (We later broke the bread and drank the warm beer.)

— * —

In 2018, one night, I wrote this silly poem for a lark, describing our encounter that eventful night of the May Day weekend in Russia in 1994. It follows the style and poetic form of Robert Service's famous poem, "The Cremation of Sam McGee."

Ode to May Day Mayhem '94

There are strange things done, and it's certainly not fun,
when you encounter the frosts of Siberia.
When the ladies are dancing, the Russians get antsy,
with their booze, their broads, and their hysteria.

The tale I tell, is sure as Hell,
it happened in '94.
A fight took charge, when a man of "large,"
took on "Tiny," on the restaurant floor.

I was there to see, the others made three,
of Canadians to see the brawl.
Our foe was daunting, as he continued his taunting,
to big Bob, six feet ten inches tall.

It started at first, when we quenched our thirst,
at the restaurant of 65.
But, by the end of the night, we were in for a fight,
as we watched our asses to stay alive.

The Russians were there, and "us" Canadians to share,
a place to have a good time.
But when the ladies came, we weren't to blame,
since friendship was not a crime.

As the evening wore on, the lines were drawn,
and the Russian showed us his ire.
But it was big Bob that claimed, in his glory to fame,
"I'll show you I'm the bigger liar."
(Pardon the pun.)

The Russian stood up, only as tall as a pup,
and announces with a growl.
"I'm the mighty Bear, and you should all beware,
that I'm on my nightly prowl."

Well, Bob arose, to his little foe,
and announces with a grin.
"I'm just like you, a Bear, that makes two,"
as he lied a little sin.

As Boris paused, now without a cause,
and hands were drawn to shake.
The fight was averted, and we were all converted,
to celebrations of vodka and cake.

The ladies danced on, as the singer sang songs,
and toasts were given with grins.
Neither fiend, nor foe, but our faces all aglow,
of friendships, vodkas, and gins.

Although it was still light, as the sun stayed the night,
we headed for home to unwind.
Where rummy was played, and beer displayed,
on the chair for the one left behind.

Larry Ritco
May 15, 2018

CHAPTER 7
REINDEER SLEDS & REFLECTIONS OF NADYM

Monday May 2
Day 6

I had a rather relaxing day in Nadym and slept until about 11:00am. Group had a short meeting in our room updating us. We expect to fly out tomorrow morning at 10:30am via helicopter. The weather today is about freezing. There was wet snow or light rain most of the day. Ray and I went for a long walk this afternoon. Then we slept, listened to Russian music on the radio, scanned our work notes on this project, or studied our Russian-English dictionaries. A couple of kids walked over to us on our walk and talked a bit even though none of us could understand each other too well. I had a Nutribar and a couple of granola bars for brunch. For supper, we took the usual two-kilometer walk to Restaurant 65. I suppose "65" stands for the 65th parallel. I think 66 degrees latitude is where the Arctic Circle starts. We saw a couple of reindeer sleds and reindeer after supper. Ray took a picture of me beside them. I didn't get too close because I figured I might spook them. With them not being tied, and the owners not around, I had visions of them running down the street with some very angry Russians chasing me. Eva served us the usual carrot, cucumber, and tomato salad, followed by the main course of sauerkraut and perhaps veal. I gave her a souvenir pin. She expressed thanks and happiness to us through sign language, as we told her we were leaving. No rowdies at the restaurant tonight. We played our usual crazy rummy tonight. I'm on a losing streak. I also lost to the computer in chess this afternoon. Overall, it was a relaxing day. [My CDN$50 RadioShack computer chess has sixteen levels of difficulty. I played at the middle level, number eight, throughout my trip to Russia.]

And, to think that we are getting paid for this. Tomorrow should be exciting as we leave to Labytnangi and possibly the site. We will always have pleasant memories of the restaurant as Eva always expected us and served us as if family. We didn't request anything; she just brought the dishes and served us well. Signing off. Do svidaniya (until we meet again) Nadym. PS Peter 1 from Holland is out chasing (Olga) Russian woman again tonight. Footnotes: We are at the Hotel Polynara. The beds are too short for us. Pillows are heavy and humongous and weigh about twenty pounds each. Rip in handbag is up to twelve inches. I will lighten it though. No problem.

Tuesday May 3
Day 7

This was a rather nice, cool day with temperature about + 5C, mostly clear, and slightly windy. At 10:00am, Lela came as expected. The bus was supposed to pick the six of us up, including the ten Russians from the drilling crew. I gave Lela a souvenir pin and thanked her for her tour the other day. Flight via helicopter was supposed to be at 11:00am. However, there was a change of plans as Lela informed us that we couldn't go today (for whatever reason). We had to haul all our suitcases back upstairs. Then we waited for about one hour to determine our status. We were then told to go and board the bus. Alexander Zubov from Amiga was also there. We all headed to the airport and unpacked. There we waited. Finally, word came that the helicopter would leave at 2:00pm. We had lunch at the cafeteria (I had noodles, tea, hamburger, and a cheese bun). Alexander paid for us (i.e. the Russian government). Then, after waiting, we were told we had to go back to the hotel. The Russians, essentially, loaded their drilling things onto the helicopter and would mobilize either this afternoon or the next day. We are to stay put until May 5th. Then, we would fly to Labytnangi and possibly see the laboratory.

The helicopter trip we were supposed to take today reminds me of my Aunt Ollie, who lives in New Westminster, B.C.

At the age of 88, she faithfully buys a lotto 649 ticket every Friday, in hopes of winning the jackpot. She keeps telling us that if she wins, the first thing she would do, after donating most of it to her relatives, friends, and charity, and which she has never done before in her life...is to go on a helicopter ride. That's still her hope and dream!

Drilling would start around May 6th at the Flox station (Ural) and approximately May 8th at the Victoria station (Yamal). We headed back to the hotel along with Ard Doorduyn and Ronald Aartsee. Ard is the OTC (observation team coordinator) and Ronald is the LC (logistics coordinator). Both are from the company Heerema in Leiden. They were in Labytnangi for a few days and they said they were bored out of their minds. They briefed Bob at the airport and will stay with us until the 5th and then head back to Moscow and then Leiden. All of us, except Ray, went for a walk and explored the many shops they have. At 5:00pm, a man from Amiga, Mr. Famienko, came and we had a meeting along with Arthur (he interprets but is also on the drilling crew) and Lela. He updated us and answered any questions. I made another batch of water using water purification tablets. The water turns brown, but tastes okay. I had some bread and cheese in John and Bob's room. We are resting now until our half hour walk to Restaurant 65. It doesn't open until 8:00pm. Chow!

This was our first introduction to Arthur. From here on in, he will take over interpreting duties from Lela. Tall, with short black hair, he wore green army fatigues. If we were at war, he would be the first one picked off since he didn't exactly blend in with the surrounding, all white environment the north offered us; but at least he stood out if we had some sort of accident and needed rescuing. He looks somewhat like Ed Chigliak (but without the long hair), the character name of a mild mannered, rather shy, Indian in the television show Northern Exposure that aired during the early-nineties. I actually did get to see Darren Burrows who played Ed, along with the rest of the cast, when they were filming in Roslyn, Washington. Since this was one of my favorite shows, I drove down there and stayed a couple days watching them film. Pretty cool stuff! I was also able to see one of the other stars up close, Jeanine Turner, considered at the time to be in the top one hundred of the most beautiful women in the world.

Surprisingly, although Ed's character is meek and mild, in person I found Darren to be quite intimidating. He is quite tall, and with a leather jacket on, I wouldn't want to meet up with him in a dark alley. He hulked over everyone else.

"Hurry up and wait!" again became the theme today as our trip to Labytnangi was called off. The pace of life in Russia, including their work efforts, isn't up to par with the western world. Delays, poor planning, and perhaps just apathy, is a norm here. We'll just have to put up with this. In this case, probably the helicopter pilot wasn't quite up to snuff, and didn't feel like flying, so we will have to sit tight.

It reminded me of the time when a man walks into a car dealership in Russia, and, after looking around, finds the car of his dreams. He proceeds to do the paperwork with the dealer. The dealer reminds him that with all the bureaucracy and red tape involved, it would actually take about ten years before he will receive the car.

"That's fine," he says. "I'm not in a rush."

After spending most of the afternoon doing paperwork, signing numerous documents, and handing over the deposit, the dealer proudly announces that he may pick his car up on May 19, 2028 (this being 2018).

"That's fine with me. Should I pick it up in the morning or afternoon?" he asks.

The dealer is kind of taken aback. "But what difference does it make? That's ten years from now."

The customer replies, "Oh, it's just that I happen to have a plumbing appointment that afternoon."

— * —

At the evening supper, Eva was mildly surprised, but happy, that we were back, after we told her yesterday we would be leaving. With her limited English she told us that she would be closed the next day. This will be our last supper here.

A few quiet customers occupied some of the tables, a huge contrast to the festivities from two days ago. Everyone seemed tuckered out, including ourselves. Our mood was a bit sombre, not much talking, perhaps a bit reflective. We weren't overly excited about leaving tomorrow, because, as always throughout this trip, itineraries change and delays occur frequently. We quietly assured ourselves that we'd be leaving. In some ways, we were anxious to get going to the site and get our feet wet, so to speak, as far as work went. We once again assumed this would be our final goodbye to Eva. In this case, it ended up being just that.

Our ritualistic 8:00pm meal was brought to us fifteen minutes later by her and consisted of roast chicken, cucumber and tomato slices, pickled cabbage or sauerkraut, beer, and coffee.

After the fine meal, we said our final "do svidaniya" and "pozhaluysta" to her. She returned the pozhaluysta to us as well, bowing graciously. We will always have many fine memories of this restaurant, not only of the good food that she served us, but also, of the fun and exuberance that everyone had a couple nights ago with our Russian comrades and (mafia?) foe.

We had our usual midnight rummy game. Peter 1 is off chasing Russian women again. Our fridge continues to shake and rumble each time it turns off. Do svidaniya. PS the hotel is starting to look not too shabby. You start to adapt to the character and age of the place. I think Calgary is going to be boring when we get back.

Wednesday May 4
Day 8

The beds we sleep in are very small, less than six feet. Poor Bob. Got up about 9:00 this morning and went for a walk around the city with Ray. It was a sunny, beautiful, windless morning, about -5C.

Bob and John went to the park and tried out the GPS today. It is a very simple device. It is hand held, and it connects with satellites to determine exact latitude and longitude. It is survey equipment which ties into a satellite to determine exact position. We need this to establish if the bench marks at the site are where they are supposed to be.

We also have our satellite phone, which we can contact Leiden, Holland to get or receive messages and thus send information back to the Calgary office. Ard also went to an Amoco office which is here in the city. Amoco is an American based oil company (I think) that has an office here and is working on some pipelines in the Yamal Region. Ard was able to procure their helicopter services in the event of an accident or emergency. They would probably be working only about fifty to one hundred miles away. Footnotes: the two Peters are from Delft, a university, not Heerema.

Today, all the car traffic is back. People must have returned to the city to start working after the four- day holiday. I came back and had some granola bars, a Nutribar, and some brown water (iodine makes it brownish). Had some cheese and bread at John and Bob's room, then went back and studied some more Russian and some work related texts. I took a nap. Then all of us, except the two Peters, went with Lela to the bank. I bought a camera (35mm) as a backup. Cost me 7,400 rubles (US$4.50). It actually gave great pictures. [I eventually gave it away to someone back home.] *Also bought a loaf of bread for about ten cents I believe. The bread was heavy and hard, but actually pretty good without butter. I had some bread and water tonight.*

We went out for supper (eight of us) to the Severyanka, a hotel and restaurant owned as well by Gazprom. The other restaurant was closed. It is quite nice, small but luxurious. It is a place for the upper class. A small group from another table gave us a bottle of brandy and toasted us to Pascho [probably Passover or Easter], *some sort of festival. We had cucumber and tomato slices, fish, chicken, pierogis, beer (pivo), coffee, some sort of chocolate marshmallow cookies, and candies. Again, Ard paid for it. Tomorrow, our helicopter flies to Labytnangi (earplug time as they are apparently quite loud). Ard said they had twenty people, cargo, and supplies in their helicopter. It must be a huge helicopter. Footnote: Seen a poster in a window that I lusted after that I think was advertising some sort of festival. It was a great traditional Siberian/Russian poster. It had a set of reindeer and a sleigh and beside it were four beautiful women in white fur coats, fur hats (shapka ushanka) and boots, with the Siberian wilderness behind them. They look stunning in them and probably 90% of women wear them. Some men have them too. Grocery stores, if you find one, actually have lots of food; cheap too. There are many people buying, and the lineups are perhaps like ours, nothing out of the ordinary. But then, the cities up North may be a bit richer than the rest due to the oil and gas industry. Dobroy nochi (good night).*

CHAPTER 8
THE LONELY ROAD

Thursday May 5. 5:51pm.
Day 9

We are now in Labytnangi, one step closer to the site. Approximately -5C, clear and pleasant. After saying goodbye to Ard Doorduyn and Ronald Aartsee at the hotel in Nadym (they were flying home to Moscow, then Amsterdam), we went to the airport with Arthur and Mr. Famienko. After setting off the alarms through security with just about everything (key chains, belt buckles, boot eyelets), we boarded a rather smoky, dirty helicopter with our luggage with eight of us, plus two or three others, probably not related to us. We all crammed in, cargo in the middle, and benches on the sides, and put our ear plugs on. The Russians didn't have any. Helicopters are quite loud. But we managed to get off the ground and make the one and a half hour trip to Labytnangi. We arrived approximately 11:00am. We didn't fly too high, only about five hundred feet I estimate. Trip was smooth and rather uneventful and too noisy to talk. Once there, we were bused to the hotel. It is very nice. Lots of wooden interior and exterior walls, carpets, clean new furniture, and beautiful light decorations. Bathrooms are two stalls and two sinks. No shower facilities, but not bad. I had a one hour rest before lunch. Lunch was in a special room for us with the food all laid out for us. It was a very nice display. I would say this is a 4 or 5 star hotel. After eating, we rested until 4:00pm, when Arthur took us on a walking tour of the town, shops, and a flea market. The town is more of a town compared to Nadym. Nadym was a concrete jungle. Labytnangi is older, but has more houses, wooden structures, tin houses, more color, less high-rises, and less beautiful women. Overall, we seem to like it more, but the Russians like Nadym better (at least Lela and Arthur). Arrived back at the hotel and will have supper at 7:00pm and a meeting with Mr. Famienko at 8:00pm. Konets. [End].

After Bob's meeting with Mr. Famienko this evening concerning the project details, Arthur and Roman, the manager of the laboratory, came here to see if the laboratory observer (me) would like to visit the lab. Despite looking forward to having a nice relaxing evening with the boys, having a beer, and playing crazy rummy, I had to go. This is what I'm paid good money for. It's my job and duty. But, just the same, when it's ten o'clock at night, after a long day of travelling and you are just settling in, the last thing you want to do is go off with a stranger and go to work. Of course, I said yes and packed my suitcases quickly. I would be staying the night there.

— * —

Roman and I leave the hotel with my suitcases in tow and trudge silently along a flat dirt road, as the sun gently tries to set in the west. The night is in a semi-twilight, a long lasting one, as complete darkness doesn't really take over until later, and then, only briefly.

After twenty minutes of walking, we stop at a lonely, deserted bus stop in the middle of nowhere. At this point my only thoughts are that I want to be anywhere, but here. I am grumpy!

The nearest houses are a couple of blocks behind us and widely scattered, haphazardly, across the plain. This really is a lonely wilderness. The community seems wrongly built and out of place as there is nothing here but a low lying, sandy landscape with a few small grass areas and scrub brush.

The minutes tick by slowly. I hear the odd rustle of the grasses as the wind picks up on occasion, its restlessness, symbolizing my evening so far. It is cool, but not that cold. I am wearing my blue jacket of medium warmth and insulation, and it has been fine for me up to this point. My heavy tan colored parka has not been used yet on this trip.

There isn't much talking between Roman and myself. What is there to say? His English is very limited and other than *Spasibo* and *Pozhaluysta* (thank you, you're welcome), I don't know any Russian. I carried all my luggage with me from the hotel and now it is sitting in front of me, as we stand, waiting for the bus. I should have left most of it at the hotel and just brought my carry-on with toothbrush and toiletry articles, but I wasn't thinking. Now I have to lug it onto and off the bus.

Another twenty minutes goes by and still there is no bus. I don't know if Roman knows what the schedule is like in this dreary, forsaken land, but it's probably infrequent. I have no idea how far the lab is. All I know is that I'll stay the night there. Bob and the boys, through some form of transportation from our Russian counterparts, will come and pick me up in the morning.

As I gaze over the grasslands, with their similar features to our prairies, I am reminded of the wolves and coyotes back home. I remember the wolves and their haunting howls as they communicate to each other in loneliness, and the coyotes with their eerie yelps and distant cries, perhaps telling everyone where the next supper is, or perhaps in loneliness, calling out to a mate.

A feeling of loneliness and despondency comes over me. I would have to say that at this moment, I reach the loneliest and lowest point of my life, standing here at a deserted bus stop in the barren Siberian landscape, with a total stranger leading me to who knows where.

I ask myself, why am I here in Russia? Why did I leave my nice comfortable setting I had back in Calgary, with its nine-to-five boring, but well established routine, where I knew what to expect for the day, and then head home to the nice comforts of my duplex, with its television, entertainment, and abundance of food that our modern society provided me with?

Uncertainty and self-doubts set in. Until now, I was having a great time with the boys, living a life of adventures with no real responsibilities and getting paid to do nothing but travel, play crazy rummy, and drink beer late into the night. We did things as a group, and I didn't have to think independently. It was going great. Other than some brief note taking about the project, most of my work still lay ahead, at both the drilling sites and this laboratory in Obskaya.

But now, it is the turning point of the trip for me. It's time to get to work and do the job that the Russian government is handsomely paying me for. It's been long overdue. I just hope I will be up to this challenge and do the job well. It's also time for me to get acquainted with my fellow Russian co-workers that I will be working alongside.

My thoughts of "self-pity" are ended when, out of the corner of my eye, I see an old bus in the far distance making its way slowly along the gentle, winding road towards us. This must be our bus. Roman says something in Russian to me, along with some gestures. I grunt my response to him even though I have no idea what he is talking about. At this point, I am just too tired to care.

We took the bus and arrived at the lab in Labytnangi 5, [a section of Obskaya] *about 18 kilometers away. I spent two hours with Roman observing and listening to him. He spoke a little English. His assistant Tatyana and two other technicians were there. I took lots of pictures. I stayed there the night at their spare bedroom. There is an outhouse. Dogs barked all night. I stayed up until 12:30 listening to Roman's theories on triaxial testing, which was totally over my head. In the morning, I was taken by jeep back to the hotel.*

CHAPTER 9
REFLECTIONS

As I reflect upon my journey so far, the phrase "Hurry up and wait," was the common theme. "Prepare to leave for the airport this morning," only to be followed up a few hours later by the words, "Wait until tomorrow," followed later by, "Perhaps the day after." Pack your suitcases, unpack your suitcases, bring them downstairs, and then bring them back up.

I reflect upon all the people we've met along the way, from our driver host in Moscow, to our hosts in Murmansk, to Lela the interpreter in Nadym, and the occasional meetings and updates with our Russian counterparts. I remember the long, refreshing walks we had to local small town restaurants, the May Day festive atmosphere we encountered in our brouhaha with the locals and their gals, and then, the sheer boredom of sitting in the hotel rooms eating granola bars, drinking iodine anointed brown water, and reading the one and only book I had, a Louis L'Amour western entitled *Comstock Lode*.

And now, how can I forget this long, lonely walk I have with a stranger, walking into the Siberian sunset, waiting for that old bus to pick us up and take us to the laboratory many kilometers away, when, all I wanted to do at this moment was to be back at the comforts of the hotel.

This lonely walk reminds me of my daily walk in life with all its difficulties. Perhaps I could simply sum it up as the ABCs of my life. They would stand for *Alone, Bored,* and *Cold.*

It seems like I have always been *cold* most of my life. I'm certainly not a winter or ocean type person. A hot desert and dry climate will suit me just fine. Yet, here I am up in the Arctic. Go figure. Perhaps it's because I was born in

December, in the middle of winter, and the house that my parents just finished building had its oil furnace installed the day before I was born. So, instead of living in a nice toasty house for the first few months of my life, it was spent under an armful of blankets, trying to stay warm.

I remember the hot summer months growing up in the Okanagan where our parents would occasionally take my two older sisters and me to Tucelnuit Lake in Oliver for a swim, and I would be freezing to death. Marlene and Debbie would be splashing around, having the times of their lives, and I would be standing there, knee deep in water, arms crossed against my chest, shivering away.

In high school, as part of the *Community Recreation* course, we went for a swim at the public swimming pool. I took the mandatory quick dip and spent the rest of the bus trip back, shivering away in my seat, actually to the point of nausea. Back at the school, I had one more class to attend to before the day was out. This was the first, and only time in my life, I skipped class on purpose because I had to spend it in the washroom with nausea and uncontrollable shivering. It took me the full hour before I actually warmed up to the point of feeling normal again.

Boredom always seemed to play a big part of my life as well. Even here, on our trip so far, the popular slogan is "Hurry up and wait." We hurry to get prepared for something, only to find out it's been delayed. Then we sit there, bored, waiting for the word before we can move on to the next adventure.

As a child, every Saturday I would go to Penticton with my mom and self-same sisters to go shopping for a couple of hours. I would buy my penny and nickel candy at the five and dime store in about five minutes flat. I was hungry and that weekly allowance money that mom doled out was burning a hole in my pocket! Besides, I didn't want inflation to set in and reduce my spending power. Then, I would wait for an hour and fifty-five minutes back at the car for the women to finish their shopping.

At school, I was always bored. I was the official clock-watcher, sitting at my desk, making sure the second and minute hands were synchronized with the corresponding bell, which signalled the end of class or lunchtime. Then I was out the door to play our made-up game of *hoc-soc*, a combination of soccer and hockey, with the goalie able to throw the ball to any of his teammates. Although any small ball, other than an actual soccer ball was used, it usually was a softball. Of course there were a lot of sore feet and shins afterwards from striking or being hit by the ball, but that was all part of the fun.

Then there is being *alone* which is part of everyone's life, especially when he or she gets old. It seems like your life starts off with a pyramid of friends, the base wide the first few years, then narrows as you get older (or if you want to think two dimensionally, a triangle with a broad base at the bottom and narrow point at the top).

Early life is teeming with friendships and friends from school, neighbours, social activities, sports, clubs, relatives including aunts, uncles, cousins, grandmas, grandpas, and then you get old. Everyone either goes to greener pastures or simply die off. They marry, change jobs, change cities, and soon you are left alone, sitting in an old folk's home.

Then the cycle repeats itself from your early years of school, and once again, you become the official clock-watcher. But this time, instead of sitting at your school desk, you are sitting in your rocking chair, watching the second and minute hands do their stuff. And, instead of looking forward to the greener pastures and fields of the hoc-so field, you are faced with the reality that the final bell is signalling you to greener pastures from beyond this earth.

You don't see your family, friends or relatives anymore, and nobody comes to visit you. You are alone. The reason why no one visits you, is not because they are too lazy, or they can't be bothered, or because they don't know where you are; the real reason they don't visit you, is because...well...they're all dead! They have died of old age.

The people who aren't that bright, and fail first or second grade repeatedly, perhaps nine or ten times, have a greater advantage over us. When they are old and in an old folk's home, most of their fellow classmates (at least the ones that they *finally* graduate with to the next grade), will be, in this scenario, about nine or ten years younger than them. For that reason, most of them will still be alive. And if the dummies (sorry, I guess I should be politically correct and say "intellectually challenged") are still on good terms with their buddies, then, their final years on this earth will be filled with an abundance of classmates and friends visiting them.

Darn that Miss Ogston for reluctantly passing me in grade two. Little was she to know, she would be narrowing my friendship base for the latter years of my life.

But I did pass grade two the first time, like everyone else, and now here I am. And both this journey to Russia and in my life has been great! Like they say, it's not the destination, but rather, the journey that counts, and so far it has been an adventurous one, albeit boring at times. You take the highs with the lows. But I wouldn't miss this for the world.

Throughout this trip, I have enjoyed everything so far and have considered this to be a blessing from God, including the sometimes questionable safety records of the air transportation I travelled on. Despite the smoke coming from the engines, or the strange noises they made, or even the possibility that some of the pilots, or co-pilots, weren't quite up to par from their party going tendencies from the previous night, I had complete faith and enjoyment. There is only so much you can do on your part, including prayer, as far as safety and protection goes, so there is no use worrying about what may or may not happen. It's in God's hands.

CHAPTER 10
NORTHERN AFFAIRS & UNCLE PETE

The stories about the Arctic regions of the North with its people and unique culture of living in a land of extremes, with its harsh environment, have always fascinated me. From the somewhat *embellished* styles of the great Canadian writer and environmentalist Farley Mowat, whose fiction and nonfiction writings center upon the Yukon and Northwest Territories, to the poetic, *witty* tales of Robert Service and his legendary poem "The Cremation of Sam McGee," the Far North is displayed with all its quirkiness. From the colorful displays of the Aurora Borealis in its nightly playful performance it gives across the skies, to the twenty-four hours a day of either sheer blackness of night or full daylight where the sun never sets; from the bitter cold of winter and its icy chills, to the short, hot summers where the air is so thick with mosquitos and black flies, both man and beast have been known to go mad to the point of insanity. From all these, legends have been made, and dramatized, into poems and tales.

Up until now, I have never had the chance to go up North, or for that matter, into the Arctic regions of the world, but I know a few people who have. One of them is my friend, Ken Baigent, from Ontario. Ken has had the great opportunity to work in Yellowknife and experience firsthand its charms. He works as a semi-government consultant educating people on energy conservation programs and government grants that are available from the federal government for businesses and individuals who own homes.

Another person who has had the privilege to travel to these remote places is my cousin George Ritco from Vancouver. He has gone overseas in the past few years to Russia, Poland, and Ukraine to visit our Ritco relatives there, and in part, to finish working on our family tree.

And then there is my Uncle Pete. Now living in Oliver, B.C., my hometown, Pete has worked in the Yukon during the sixties doing geotechnical surveys and feasibility studies and looking for ore deposits for a mining company.

His story telling and yarns of years gone by continue to fascinate me, although, as his memory fades, they have a tendency to change slightly, towards the point of embellishment. As an example, Pete and I like to go to Penticton on occasion for a drive, and since we are there, check out the casino to see what's happening. In addition, since there is no point in driving back home without going on a bit of a diet and losing a bit of weight (i.e. from our wallets) we usually decide to test out the machines to see if they are working properly. Most times, they aren't, but that doesn't really matter. Sometimes they do work quite well. Pete was telling me the other day that his good friend Dorothy Mellon phoned him to say she won big at the casino. She was playing the $1.80 slots, won $1,800, and had to brag about it. So, of course, every time I saw Pete over the next few weeks, and since his short term memory is poor, he would relate to me, over and over, that same old story about her winnings. Finally, after a few weeks, his story suddenly changed. Each time I see him now, he tells me that Dorothy phoned him to tell him she won *$18,000* at the casino playing the $1.80 slots. I reminded him that the number he gave me was $1,800 a while ago, but he insists its $18,000. I tried to tell him that the slots probably don't pay out that much, but Pete doesn't believe me. So far, it's been a few months, and that number has remained constant and hasn't changed. After all, even in Pete's mind, I think that $180,000 would be inconceivable and too far-fetched to be believed. [Actually, to update you, the latest figure that Pete insists upon now that is correct, is $14,000.]

We had a recent adventure together in a small town, and, although it wasn't in the Arctic or the northern regions, we experienced that same rugged, independent spirit and character from its people that you would find up North. It is a town full of character and characters.

Greenwood, B.C is recognized as the smallest incorporated city in Canada with a population of about seven hundred. As a former mining town, it was well known as a principle city in the boundary country district for its copper smelting and mining from 1896 to 1910. However, it has been in decline ever since. Miners and prospectors, once in abundance, are now long gone. But occasionally, some old geezers can still be found sitting outside the local store on its wooden verandah. Old wooden buildings still stand on Main Street filled with relics and sold in the form of antiques, in reflections of a bygone era.

In the summer of 2017, Pete and I drove to Grand Forks, B.C. to visit the Ritco clan for a family BBQ. On the way back, Pete needed to get some salt, but also figured to purchase a lotto 649 ticket at the same time. He figured that the more towns you visit for the purchases, the higher your chances of winning would be, so we stopped into Greenwood. This, according to Pete's logic, was supposed to be the birthplace of the ticket to Canada's next millionaire. (Actually, we came close. Of the two tickets we bought, we won a free ticket. At least it was a step in the right direction.)

As Uncle Pete and I got out of the car, I immediately noticed seven or eight old timers, sitting in wooden rocking chairs on the store's front verandah, glaring at us with steely eyes. As the hot afternoon sun shone down on us, they rocked away in the shade to the delightful shrieks and creaks of their rockers. Flies buzzed around their rugged, bearded faces as they occasionally hesitated, as if in doubt, whether to spit, or bother to swat the "little buggers." Surprisingly, some still had some of their teeth. Some wore dusty, old moth-eaten hats. They took their eyes off us only long enough to finally make a decision, bend down, and spit on the wooden slats that their feet rested upon. They still had gumption. If only Festus was here.

We entered the store and what happened next, I will tell, in the form of a poem I wrote about Uncle Pete. This is his life story, especially the last eighteen years.

Good Old Uncle Pete

Pete was his name, his claim to fame,
was reading the massive books.
Mr. Crucetti had owned, and to Pete he had loaned,
the books from the restaurant's cooks.

Twelve volumes in all, they weren't very small,
he read from A to Z.
Encyclopedia it said, and Pete he read,
apples to oranges to zzzzz's.

Six years it took, of the loans from the cooks,
minus about seventy-seven dates.
History he learned, from all of Nero's burns,
and to Alexanders and the Greats.

But bingo was his game, for glory or shame,
to the city of Penticton afar.
Forty kilometers to make, past Skaha Lake,
he drove his sleek black car.

Starting with Monday, but never on Sunday,
six days a week he went.
To this bingo show, to his later woes,
of hard earned money spent.

In O.K. Falls, he answered the calls,
to cheezies and a pint of beer.
Then off he'd go, being careful and slow,
to avoid the police so near.

Each week of the year, cold winters no fear,
his Malibu he would faithfully take.
When the dreams of the call, when the machine dropped the ball,
"BINGO"
of the money that he would probably make.

The lady there, was friendly and fair,
and soon a bond was "a tellin."
Dorothy was her name, call her "Dot" just the same,
but her last name was the same as a melon.

The years went by, and Pete started to cry,
of all lost monies spent.
"Don't worry about that," I said with a spat,
"Consider it money well lent."

"To keep the place going, and the money 'a flowing,'
you were able to play for years.
But now it has chosen, for the bingo hall to 'a closing,'
and now you can shed your tears."

One day Pete and I, had a coffee and pie,
and made a summer plan.
To Grand Forks we'd go, to Shirley's café for a "Joe,"
then off to the Ritco clan.

BBQ and gins, shirts and skins,
it was a happy and joyous day.
Thank George, Robin, and all, who had answered the call,
and the clan who put on the display.

On the way back, Pete saw a shack,
in Greenwood as we passed thru.
"I need some salt, and thought we could halt,
and get some lotto tickets too."

Well Pete got his salt, and it wasn't his fault,
but a lady fell for him.
She swerved and feinted, as if slightly tainted,
by some beers, or tonics, or gins.

Pete held her tight, she was a mighty sight,
and asked her how she was.
She looked up high, up to the skies,
and said after a pause.

"I see the mighty Lord, and the flaming sword,
and I know I should not lie.
Perhaps it's meant, that I have to feint,
when in the arms of handsome guys."

The old storekeeper lady, rather dark and shady,
on seeing Myrtle with men.
She says, "Hey a Myrtle? ...Are you a flirting?
with all of the guys again?"

The gig was done, and she was gone,
through the doors of the former saloon.
Past the ancient miners, who sat in modern recliners,
and spat in spit-polished spittoons.

Larry Ritco
March 16, 2018

This poem is mostly true and reflects upon my Uncle Pete accurately. Mr. Crucetti, who owns a restaurant in Oliver, *did* have an encyclopedia set which he loaned to Pete back in the sixties. Pete was in his late thirties with back problems and couldn't work at the time, so every night he would read one of the volumes that he took home. Starting off with volume A, it took him five years, nine months and thirteen days (he still remembers that time length) to completely read the entire encyclopedia set. He told me that, after reading for hours each night, starting what the "A" volume, perhaps of naked, Amazonian jungle women and bronzed warriors with spears, he would proceed to have vivid dreams of them chasing him through the jungles of Brazil. If he was in volume B, he would be dreaming about black bears chasing him up trees in B.C. I'm sure by the time he got to volume Z those pesky striped horses would be chasing him through the deserts of Africa.

For eighteen years, Pete drove his car to Penticton, forty kilometers away, to play bingo six days a week and dropping in O.K. Falls on the way back for a cheezie and beer. He took Sundays off; not that he is a religious person he just felt he needed a day of rest (probably from his losses). In addition, he did meet a woman whom, over the years, he became great friends with, whose name was Dorothy, nicknamed "Dot," Mellon.

He kept track of his losses, and I won't say how much they were, other than it was in the "many" tens of thousands of dollars. However, as the poem says, he alone, probably kept the bingo hall going for years before it finally closed its doors in 2017.

That same year, we went to Grand Forks, and on the way there, stopped into my cousin Shirley and her husband Scott's restaurant, *The Trading Post*, in Rock Creek. They had bought it a few years earlier. She wasn't there, but we talked to her daughter Amber and had a coffee and juice.

Later that afternoon, the Ritco clan put on a terrific BBQ at Ron Ritco's place, and I met my relatives, many of whom I hadn't met before, or only when I was very small. My dad Dick, Aunt Ollie, and Uncle Pete were all born there.

On the way back, in Greenwood, we stopped at a store for Pete to get his salt. After getting a lotto ticket as well, and I, graciously allowing him to buy me one too (I didn't need any salt), Pete and I headed for the door. A woman perhaps in her fifties came in, and literally *swooned* into my/Pete's arms. (Actually, she was in my arms, but that is beside the point and it screws up the poem with its emphasis on Pete.) She did appear to faint as if she had a medical issue, so Pete and I were both quite concerned.

Nevertheless she replied, looking at Pete (it was Pete she was looking at), "I always do this when I'm in the presence of handsome men." Pete is actually quite handsome, even at the age of ninety; still has most of his hair, slicked back, that Italian mafia look.

The storekeeper behind us then yelled out, "Mirtle, are you flirting with the customers again?" We all had a good laugh.

Out the doors, we carefully skirted the wet spots the old men had laid at their feet. The occasional spittle came our way, perhaps just to spite us and amuse themselves for albeit what little entertainment they have these days.

Though Greenwood may be the smallest incorporated city in Canada, it has real character and characters...and I like it! Our lives were enriched by those moments we spent there. And to think, we wouldn't have stopped in Greenwood, except for the need of the one necessity to all life - "Salt." (And a lotto 649 ticket.)

— * —

Getting back to the poem "The Cremation of Sam McGee" by Robert Service, I decided to write a parody of it.

The Creation of Ham McGhee

There are strange things done, in the midnight sun,
by the ones who broil your burgers.
The yellow arches, have their secret marches,
of tales of burger mergers.
The Northern Lights, have seen queer sights,
but the queerest they ever did see.
Was that night of the blizzard, he merged ham and gizzard,
he created the Ham McGhee.

Now Sham McGhee, was from Appellee, came from land of cotton blooms.
Why he left his home, in the South to roam, we can only guess and assume.
He was always sold, of an arch of gold, that seemed to hold him like a spell.
Though he would often say, in his homely way, his burgers "Were sure (as hell)
    to sell."

On a Christmas Day, we were munching our way, through awesome
    meat entrails.
Talk of your bold, through eyes that's sold, we told him not to fail.
If our eyes we'd close, our hopes were froze, our dreams we couldn't see.
It wasn't much fun, but the only one to glimmer, was Sham McGhee.

And that very night, as we packed in tight, burgers beneath the dough.
Our bellies were fed, and the stars o'er head, were dancing heel and toe.
He turned to me and "Cap," says he, "I'll cash this flip I guess.
And if I do, I'm asking that you, won't refuse my last request."

Well he seemed so high, and I didn't know why, then he says with a sort of grin.
"It's this blessed mold, and I'm sure as sold, that this mash is sure to win!
We're far ahead, and sure as led, that our goals have all been met.
So I want you to swear, that foul or fair, this is where we rest our bet."

A pal's last need, is a thing to heed, so I swore I would not fail.
And we started on, at the streak of dawn, the long exciting trail.
In the month of May, he raved every day, of home with its home cooked meals.
But by that fall, he had answered the call, and was sold on fast food deals.

Now Sham McGhee, agrees with me, that this was a lot of fun.
The mix, the mold, arches of gold, all done under the Arctic sun.
To sum it up, McGhees grew up, to become a household name.
I must admit, through shivers and s---- (fits), we crossed that threshold of fame.

But Sham grew old, and from what I'm told, he died one starry night.
In the Arctic's womb, laid in an icy tomb, he lies staring at the Northern lights.
Unlike cousin Sam, roasting like a ham, enjoying his time in hell.
Sham shall always boast, of the colorful host, he sees from God's heavenly spell.

There are strange things done, in the midnight sun,
by the ones who broil your burgers.
The yellow arches, have their secret marches,
of tales of burger mergers.
The Northern Lights, have seen queer sights,
but the queerest they ever did see.
Was that night of the blizzard, he merged ham and gizzard,
he created the Ham McGhee.

Larry Ritco
September 14, 2013
Revised November 10, 2018

Sikorsky helicopter at Labytnangi airport (helipad) prior to our final destinations to Baydaratskaya Bay. Bob Forsythe the team leader, and Arthur the interpreter, center left.

Another view of the Sikorsky helicopter.

Heading to Baydaratskaya Bay via helicopter.

The treeline below us disappearing as we head north.

Approaching Flox station on the western shores of Baydaratskaya Bay.

Baydaratskaya Bay.

The bay starting to break up.

Victoria weather station, Baydaratskaya Bay. The author, Larry Ritco, standing in front.

Sun trying to set at Victoria weather station.

Overlooking the bay. Photograph taken just behind Victoria weather station.

The sleeping quarters for everyone in camp Victoria except for the weather personnel. Larry and Ray standing in front.

Peter 1 and Ray in our sleeping quarters, upon first arrival.

Our dingy washing area.

Diesel heater and stove used to heat the shack
and for heating water for coffee or tea.

The new outhouse and generator building, with the main weather station in the background. Photo taken from near the south shoreline of the bay (Victoria station).

The same buildings as the previous photo, looking south towards the bay.

Gypsy, the castaway dog, ready to play.

Peter 1 and Ray playing cards.

Andre, a Russian driller, and Larry competing for the chess championship of the Arctic, while Peter 1 (left) reads a book.

Larry with one of the few activities in camp to keep him occupied.

Ray Hunt on Baydaratskaya Bay.

The author, Larry Ritco, on Baydaratskaya Bay.

The Canadian flag placed at its final resting place on a derelict building just outside of Victoria station.

Lunch at the Victoria station dining room. (l-r), unknown
Russian driller, Ray Hunt, Peter 1, and Bob Forsythe.

Labytnangi, (l-r). Ray, John, Michael an interpreter/
teacher, and Peter 2 in front of possibly a store.

Laboratory in Obskaya (Labytnangi).

Another view of the laboratory I think. (All the buildings looked the same!)

Salekhard Airport.

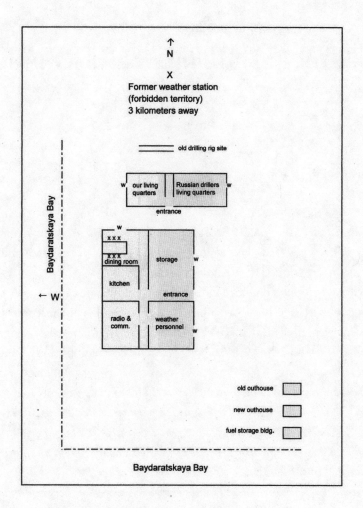

Map - Layout of Camp Victoria, Baydaratskaya Bay, Russia

CHAPTER 11
ARRIVAL AT VICTORIA WEATHER STATION

Friday May 6. 4:52pm.
Day 10

The expedition has ended. We have arrived at the Victoria site at Baydaratskaya
Bay about 3:00pm. It took us eight days and 14 hours [if my math and time
conversions are correct] *from leaving the Calgary office*

What was supposed to take us four days to get to base camp, took us nine,
using commercial airlines, cargo planes, and large Sikorsky helicopters. (No
dog sleds were needed, thankfully, otherwise it would have taken us longer.)
Weather delays and the May Day long weekend celebrations slowed us down
quite a bit.

We were supposed to leave our hotel at 10:00am, but were delayed for one
and a half hours. We jammed our things into the helicopter. It was earplug time
again. We had about twelve or thirteen people. We flew at a height between three
and five hundred feet (altimeter on board). Left about 1:00pm and arrived at
Flox station about 2:45pm. This is the Ural side of the Bay where they will do
some drilling (seventeen holes). Half of our party stopped off here and unloaded
their luggage. As they unloaded, the helicopter pilot kept the engines going to save
time. We stayed just long enough to unload them, and then, about 10 minutes
later, the pilot started to take off without Peter 1. Peter got carried away with
unloading luggage, so he almost got left behind. Ray, Peter 1, and I will go to the
Victoria station while Bob, John, and Peter 2 were dropped off here. Then it was

across the bay to Victoria station. The ice was breaking up and there were open areas. These stations are weather stations.

Earlier this morning, after a sobering safety meeting with Arthur at the hotel concerning site conditions, the six observers (four Canadians and two Dutch), flew out by Sikorsky helicopter to the weather stations. Most of the Russian drilling crew would fly in later. As we flew north, the treeline started to disappear until all that was left below us was a white, flat, snow-covered landscape.

After a few hours flying, the helicopter arrived at the Flox station on the western shoreline of Baydaratskaya Bay where half of our crew, including our boss Bob Forsythe, John Fitcher, and Peter 2 were dropped off. The drop off, including mail delivery, was brief, then off we flew across the vast frozen, but cracked, bay to the Victoria site situated on the other side. Throughout the crossing, I alternated between watching the altimeter above the cockpit door and the ice below (as if that would help), making sure we weren't losing altitude and falling into the water below us. There wasn't any backup plan, life jackets or rafts. If you go down, you go down. In these frigid conditions, survival in the sea is only a few minutes, far too short for the helicopters at the oil rigs, one hour away, to rescue us.*

I always wore my earplugs in the helicopters or planes, as they were noisy. After about twenty minutes, my confidence eroded, as I saw the altimeter drop to eighty feet and lowering. Quickly looking out the window, expecting to come face to face with the chilling waters, I was relieved to see that we were over the bay and descending to our final destination.

This is the Victoria weather station site on the eastern shoreline. It's a small outpost with a few old buildings, and skeletal structures of previously abandoned ones. About thirty kilometers (twenty miles) separates us from the first crew across the bay. These two places will be our homes for the next few weeks.

---

*Eight years later, at 7:55pm on Tuesday July 16, 2002, a Sikorsky S76A helicopter crashed into the North Sea, killing all eleven people on board. Five engineers and subcontractors were from our company AMEC (formerly HBT Agra).

The helicopter was making a routine ten-minute flight from the gas production platform *Clipper* to the drilling rig *Global Santa Fe Monarch*, when it crashed into the sea.

Upon investigation, it was discovered that one of the rotors was fractured severely. In 1999, this particular helicopter was struck by lightning from which that rotor was hit. Although the rotor was repaired, the lightning strike exploited an anomaly in the blade and damaged and weakened the spar, thus contributing to the cause of the crash.

Source: Wikipedia

www.wikipedia.org/wiki/2002_Bristow_Helicopters_Sikorsky_S_76A-crash

You never know....

CHAPTER 12
OVERVIEW OF VICTORIA WEATHER STATION

The camp itself, known as the Victoria weather station, is situated on the eastern shores of Baydaratskaya Bay. The GPS coordinates for the site are approximately 69° 0′ north and 67° 30′ east, as it lies just inside the Arctic Circle, with that being approximately 66°.

Baydaratskaya Bay is in northwestern Russia, just east of the Ural Mountains and west of the Yamal peninsula, home to some of Russia's largest oil and gas reserves.

It has extremely harsh environmental conditions where temperatures of -50C can occur in winter, and 80% of the territory is covered by lakes, swamps, and rivers.

The portion of the project we are working on is where the gas pipeline(s) will rest on the seabed as (they) cross this shallow bay, on the way to feeding Europe and meeting its gas needs. The drilling program will be done at the two critical crossings, at the shorelines, and the results we get will give a soil profile of the seabed and help determine if permafrost conditions exists. This will help the engineers in their overall design for the layout of the six proposed pipelines, as they cross this critical location. [Initial plans were for six pipelines to be laid. After the first trunk line was laid, a second trunk line was built a short time later. See the update at the end of the book.]

Since this is early May, we are experiencing mild, but cool temperatures, on average of about -5C. Our heavy parkas with fox-lined hoods, in preparation of being here earlier in winter, are a bit excessive, especially in comparison to our poor Russian co-workers who have simple overcoats and jackets.

The snow-covered terrain is flat, frozen, and treeless with no vegetation and perhaps a snow depth of one foot or so. Snowdrifts of four or five feet surround the camp buildings.

This is polar bear country. Although they are rarely seen, all individuals including the drilling crew, who leave the camp area must be escorted by someone with a shotgun. Later on, I was to disregard this rule, but thank the Lord, he protected me from my stupid decisions, and I didn't encounter any of these beasts. Apparently, they are one of the few mammals on earth that won't hesitate to stalk and kill a human being for food.

The sun sets briefly each night for a few hours, so the days are long and bright. The Canadians and the Dutch brought sunglasses to prevent snow blindness but alas, the Russians have none. After a few days here, there will be almost continuous sunlight twenty-four hours a day as the sun wanders clockwise, staying slightly above the flat, distant horizon. For this reason, the plans are to have two-twelve hour shifts, working twenty-four hours a day on the drilling program. Of course, once we got started, this never came to fruition, as typically most plans go by the wayside in Russia.

We never did see the aurora borealis (or the northern lights if you prefer) during our stay at camp Victoria, nor, for that matter, anywhere in Russia. However, I have heard that this country is a great place to see them, especially with us being so far north. Being late in the season, with the long daylight hours and milder temperatures, probably were the reasons why we never saw them. But we did see a couple of sun dogs a few times around midday, which were quite neat to see. A sundog, or mock sun, is a bright spot on either side of the sun and is caused by the refraction of sunlight by ice crystals in the air.

The North Pole has no set time zone to go by, since all twenty-four time zones dissect through it. The time zone traditionally used by travellers or workers is one found in their home country. We chose a time zone two hours earlier than Moscow although I didn't realize that initially.

Camp Victoria consists of a few old wooden and tin buildings. The main building, facing east away from the shoreline, holds the weather station facilities, communications equipment, and is the sleeping quarters for the two or three weather personnel who run it. This room is to the left as you enter the building. There is also a small kitchen and dining room at the far corner with a large main storage room at the entrance.

A small kitchen no bigger than an apartment sized kitchen will keep the cook and his assistant busy the next few weeks as they will feed the twenty-three personnel in camp.

The dining room is small, one table and six chairs. We would take turns when it came time to eat, but the Russians were kind and usually allowed Ray, Peter, and I first seating. A small window about three feet by three feet faces the bay towards the northwest and is permanently frosted up and frozen on the outside. An old, brown cloth depicting the sickle and hammer hangs on the wall near it. It will be in this room where Ray, Peter, and I alongside Arthur our interpreter, would sit many evenings as one of the Russian drillers entertained us with his fascinating Russian tales about life in Russia and his experiences and adventures. Sometimes we all partook in the discussions concerning religion, politics, world events, or sports, but more often than not, it was Mesha who would lead us with his stories, which helped melt away our cultural differences.

A large utility room, or storage area, near the front porch entry, stores all the miscellaneous stuff; outdoor gear, coats, boots, crates of food, and drilling equipment. Behind it, apparently, is a rough bathing area where, if you were ambitious enough to fetch some buckets of ice, and heat them on the stove, you could have a hot bath. There might have been a tub there, but I'm not sure. I never took a bath, nor Peter or Ray to my knowledge. I think only the Russians used these facilities. I'm sure we must have stunk pretty badly after we left camp a few weeks later.

About seventy yards southeast is a small building that houses the generator and fuel that supplies the camp with electricity and heating. I'm not sure what fuel is used for the generator, perhaps diesel, perhaps gasoline. Diesel fuel is the one used for the heaters. Sometimes the person responsible would forget to fill the heater in our living quarters, and we would have to wear our parkas and put up with a cold room until it was replenished.

In between the weather station and the generator building stands the forlorn, but much depended upon, outhouse. With four simple walls, a roof, and a hole in the ground, it is in dire need of replacement. The first hole drilled by the drilling crew would be for the new outhouse.

Twenty yards north of the weather station is the living and sleeping quarters for everyone except the weather personnel. The metal, rectangular trailer, approximately ten feet by forty feet, sits elevated a couple feet off the frozen ground on temporary wooden ties at its four corners. There is an upright ten-gallon, metal oil drum that is used as a step into the building, located halfway.

As you step up, the first thing you see is a small utility room, about five feet wide and seven feet long, with a simple sink, counter area, diesel fed heater, and a stove in it. This is the wash area, and the room is filthy by all standards. A dirty towel hangs on a nail. A few pots and pans hang on the walls, and there is a kettle for boiling water for coffee or tea. A metal cherry pail above the sink serves as the water supply container for washing. The bottom of the pail has a small hole in it where a simple plug sits with its vertical stem assembly extending downward. An upward push on the stem allows the water to pour out, and a release allows the water pressure to push down on the inside plug, thus sealing the hole. We will use the sink area for simple washing of hands and face and perhaps washing socks and underwear, but not much else. Clean ice will have to be fetched from nearby to fill the teakettle for drinking.

The drip-fed diesel heater consists of a supply tank with a metal tube extending downward to a heating basin and fire. A valve on the tube controls the drip, and thus the heating, as the drip feeds the fire.

To the left, as you enter, is the sleeping quarters for Ray, Peter 1, and I. The ten foot by twelve-foot room has one electrical outlet on one of the thinly insulated blue walls, and a naked lightbulb on the ceiling. A small window on the west side overlooks the bay. The room is sparsely furnished with two old beds, a creaky cot with a thin, dirty mattress, a small chair, and two small tables. This room would soon be home to some of the most hotly contested chess matches as Russia battled Canada: Andre versus Larry for the chess championship of the Arctic Circle. Although the current world chess champion was Russian Anatoly Karpov, the competitors would not recognize his reign in this jurisdiction. They would consider the Arctic Circle "off limits," a separate entity and not part of the rest of the world. They would be fighting for honor, glory, and valour for their respective countries. Their reputations, what little they were, were at stake.

On the right side of the building is a room approximately ten feet by twenty feet, which the Russian drillers would call their sleeping quarters. I rarely entered their room while here in camp other than the few occasions I went over to see if Andre wanted a chess game or two. The Russians kept to themselves and were quiet. Blankets nailed across the top of the doorways of both sleeping quarters provided the privacy of each section.

Further north of our living shack, about eighty yards away, are the metal skeletal remains of a former building, long since torn down and plundered. It might have been a storage shed at one time for equipment. It will be here on a lone, upright, metal pole that just prior to our departure from camp, I tie my small Canadian flag. Unfortunately, in my haste, since the helicopter might be flying in at any moment, I accidentally placed it upside down.

Three kilometers north of this site are some more derelict remains of some buildings. This may have been where the original weather station once stood. To this site, a few days into camp, I was to take my forbidden walk alone and still manage to live and talk about it. Although the bleak, white landscape is generally devoid of wildlife, the odd marauding polar bear has been known to prowl around the area in search of food.

Back in camp there is a castaway dog that the Russians have named Gypsy. She is a medium-sized dog with a black and white coat and looks somewhat like a Border collie, the kind you find rounding up sheep in Australia. She is probably bored here, since there are few sheep to tend to. No one knows where she came from, perhaps a previous weather employee owned her, or maybe a reindeer herder lost her, or left her behind. But she is friendly to everyone, and it seems her only duty in camp is to be the *official greeter* to everyone and welcome them, friend or foe (no discrimination here), and perhaps escort us to the outhouse in a particularly stormy blizzard.

In summary, Victoria weather station is lonely, remote, and primitive. It is inaccessible by boat or airplane. There are no towns for hundreds of kilometers. The lone link to the world is a helicopter that flies in sporadically approximately every three days with food, mail, and supplies. Sometimes a Russian herder with his reindeer-driven sled would come into camp and barter meat for canned goods, but otherwise, the camp is isolated. There is no television or radio for entertainment. I have only one book, a Louis L'Amour book entitled *Comstock Lode* to read, and two chess sets, including a RadioShack electronic version with sixteen levels of difficulty, to satisfy my boredom.

In the days to come, we will live off simple meals that the cook makes, consisting mainly of porridge, bread, coffee, and tea for breakfast, soup and bread for lunch, and macaroni or rice and a small amount of meat for supper.

However, unknown to Ray and Larry early on, Peter 1 has brought along a food suitcase consisting of canned goods: chili, stews, spaghetti, and meats of all sorts, a gourmet's delight (at least for a man). Later on, this cache was raided when we got desperately tired of camp food. Sometimes if an evening meal was particularly bad, we made sure to check that Gypsy was still around. She was. Tail wagging, big smile on her face, she always managed to dodge the pots and pans of the cook.

This is an all-male camp with just the one female...Gypsy...the castaway dog.

CHAPTER 13
SETTLING IN

Friday May 6 (cont.)
Day 10

The Russian Sikorsky helicopter, with its distinctive orange and black colors, landed just yards from camp on the frozen tundra. We jumped out and with the help of the two weather personnel from the station, quickly unloaded the wooden crates of supplies and our luggage. There was no time for formal introductions or bantering, just help unload everything, and get the helicopter and its pilot back in the air. Time is money with helicopters (except when the pilot doesn't show up for work due to not feeling well, of which only a tomato juice in the morning can cure).

Our SOS emergency cards almost came into play for the first time this trip as we almost got a hernia lifting Peter's suitcase off the helicopter. What on earth was in it? Up to this point, he hadn't told us what was in that pirate's treasure chest of his. His suitcase itself was ruggedly made and weighed not just a few pounds.

As we unloaded the supply crates onto sleds and toboggans, I noticed, from their labels, most contained food, much of which appeared quite promising; cookies, pastries, and an assortment of canned meats and vegetables. Moreover, there was lots of it.

"Hmmm," I thought, "we might be eating quite nicely here in camp."

Nevertheless, I was sadly mistaken. We never did partake in most of those delights. Those crates of food would have added much variety to our otherwise, bland meals, the typical "Russian camp food," that was eventually served to us. I can only guess and surmise that the good stuff was reserved for the weather personnel (and/or certain "privileged" Russians) who, when we weren't around, ate to their hearts content. Not that I was envious or harbouring any grudges towards them. It's just that I really *was* looking forward to eating those Russian pastries that were in those crates.

Even though I love my pastries, back home I rarely buy any, since I know I can't control myself. Instead, I keep a few packages of the boring digestive cookies around when I need to satisfy my cravings. Of course, they get past their "best before" date by a few years, but that doesn't matter. I can still use them whenever I have company. Along with tea, they are just fine to eat, albeit a bit stale. Nobody will notice, just as long as he or she doesn't read this section of the book!

With the helicopter now lifting off, amidst its artificially created snowstorm, and heading north to make another pickup or delivery, we dragged the fully loaded sleds to the main building, the weather station, where, at the entrance we unloaded them into the storage room. It only took us a few minutes to unload everything then was able to stop, catch my breath, and have formal introductions to everyone in camp.

But prior to this work stoppage, the first one to greet informally, but officially (since it was her duty), was Gypsy the castaway dog; albeit at this time we didn't know her name, nor that she was a castaway. With tail wagging and tongue hanging from her mouth, drooling with excitement, she paced feverishly back and forth, hoping to offer assistance of any kind as we hauled the sleds. Perhaps if she was a Husky, we would have considered her services, but she didn't meet the strength and height requirements. A few happy barks now and then confirmed to us that we were considered *friends* to her. She welcomed us with open *paws*.

As we were led into the kitchen, Arthur introduced us to Alex the cook and his assistant. I never did catch the assistant's name and rarely saw him afterwards other than the times he was in the kitchen doing prep work for our meals. Alex and he would have their hands full, as their job was to feed twenty-three hungry men three times a day.

We were also introduced to the two weather personnel who stay at and operate the station. We didn't see much of them either, during our stay, probably because they were too busy with work (or busy playing games on their computer). Most of the drillers would be coming in the next day or so, so the camp was still fairly empty.

After talking to someone briefly, Arthur led Peter, Ray, and I to an old metal trailer to the north a few yards away. This will be the aforementioned sleeping quarters for the drillers and us. We stepped out of the deep snow drifts alongside the building onto the ten-gallon drum steps that led into the metal shack and were confronted, for the first time, with the primitive heating and utility room. As we saw that this room was not a finalist, nor for that matter, even an entry level participant for any *spic and span* commercial, we realized that we would have to take a step down from our luxurious lifestyles we enjoyed back home in North America. We didn't linger long here.

As I think about the primitive, yet ingenious faucet setup in the far corner of this room, I was reminded of my two older sisters, whom I love dearly, back home. Recently, while they were visiting, the oldest one, Marlene, came to my apartment one day and had to use the bathroom. Actually, she didn't have to use the toilet facilities she just had to wash her hands, since she is a germaphobe. Not knowing how to use the one-spout faucet, she proceeded to yank the handle right off its assembly. I guess she didn't realize her strength. Sheepishly, she apologized to me and really wanted to pay for the damage she caused. Rather than taking advantage of the monetary offer she gave me, for a ten-second job of tightening a setscrew, I declined. We all had a good laugh.

Not ten minutes later, sister number two on the depth chart, Debbie Rosenau, had to go to the bathroom. She is not a germaphobe but actually did have to use the toilet facilities. Not realizing what Marlene had done previously, but with the same genetic code as sister number one (runs in the family), she continued in her footsteps and proceeded to yank my poor faucet handle off as well. As a highly emotional person that she is, and linking this situation on par to that of the Hindenburg disaster of 1937, she came out of the bathroom with tears streaming down her face, and my faucet handle in her hands. But unlike Marlene, who perhaps is better off financially, no monetary offers were given to me. We all had a good laugh over the situation although Debbie was still drying her tears when she finally was able to laugh.

Later on, a dab of epoxy glue solved the problem permanently. Although, as mentioned I love both sisters dearly, I don't trust them and plan on writing out a set of instructions as to how to use my faucet the next time they are in my apartment.

There was another story that Debbie told us when she was at a restaurant in Quesnel, B.C. and had to use the washroom again. The restaurant was somewhat of old and had a washroom door that didn't sit properly in its casing. Upon finishing her toilet duties, and washing up, Debbie tried opening the door. It was jammed. She yelled out for help, but no one heard her.

With claustrophobia setting in and starting to panic, she proceeded to heave her slightly overweight body against the door frame, neatly smashing the door off its hinges.

The owner (and cook) of the restaurant had a slightly perplexed look on his face when Debbie approached him with the smashed door in her hands.

"The door wouldn't open," were her only words.

After a few moments, when the shock subsided, the owner told her he knew for some time that that door was causing problems for his patrons and would be in need of fixing. At least now, this gave him an excuse to finally getting around to doing it.

No charges were laid against Debbie, and she didn't have to pay for damages...but she did have to return the door. I think Debbie should seriously think of becoming a Narc. She might be quite good at it. They wouldn't need to invest in a battering ram.

— * —

Moving right along, to the left of the utility room, we pushed aside our blanket door into our sleeping quarters, and dumped our luggage onto the beds. The two main beds lay perpendicular to each, occupying the far half of the room while a cot lay at the front. I volunteered to take the rickety cot with its dirty, slim mattress, since I have the least amount of work and leave the beds for Peter and Ray. The rest of the interior was austere with a few simple furniture pieces. A medium-sized table occupied the center of the room. Despite the loneliness of the one electrical outlet on one wall, I realized we didn't have many gadgets that need electricity. Our lives have now been simplified compared to the modern outside world.

Looking out the bare window, with no curtains, we saw the bay where the drilling spots were marked off with orange-flagged stakes where, in a few days, we will start the drilling program. The bedroom was cold since nobody had turned the heater on yet, and we were the first to arrive. We wandered to the Russian side of things and peeked through their blanket barrier to see who had the better accommodations. Although their room was bigger to fit the twelve drillers, the same company did the interior design. They were on a tight budget. But then again, who am I to criticize, as I stood there in my gawky, over-dressed, bulky outfit, looking like a blimp. I wouldn't win any fashion awards either. The living quarters will do.

We made our way back to the main weather station (w. s.), where Alex had prepared his daily lunch special, a thin soup consisting of macaroni and rice, with a little meat, and freshly baked, albeit heavy, white bread. As a short, thin man with grizzled beard, Alex, like any cook throughout the history of humanity, is very sensitive to his achievements in the culinary world and will not take guff from anyone. He expects us to show good conduct and manners and appreciate his work with the odd compliment sent his way from time to time. Show him respect. If we criticized his meals, we might soon find ourselves with Gypsy as our new dinner mate, eating and growling together, as we competed for food off the same plate.

We ate in silence and reflection. The feeling of separation from the rest of our six-man crew hadn't quite sunk in yet. We were still overwhelmed by our new surroundings and the whirlwind of events from the past twenty-four hours, trying to absorb it all. With the *whomp, whomp, whomp* of the Sikorsky's large rotor blades still pounding in our brains, our strained bodies and minds slowly started to unwind.

When we arrived, it was not that cold, about 0C and little wind. We met with the Russians, a grizzly looking bunch and Alex the cook. We had tea, soup, and bread. Our cabin is about ten feet by twelve feet for the three of us. It is very small, but is the warmest. It actually is quite nice out right now. The place is pretty grubby though. I expect to be here two or three days and essentially do nothing until the drilling starts. They will probably keep the lab in Labytnangi so I will probably fly back in a few days. So here I am in the Arctic Circle in or close to Siberia. Arctic Circle starts around 66 degrees latitude and we are around 69 degrees.

Our place that we stay (metal shack) is overlooking the shoreline about fifty yards away. The terrain is very flat. No trees, obviously, and a beautiful view as we see the sun still quite high and two sundogs, one on each side. It is just like you see in National Geographic magazine. We actually heard birds out here like the ones at home. It was quite windy and cold out, but with our parkas on, it was no problem at all. The drilling probably won't start until Sunday. We had a tour of the campsite and the toilet and an old drilling rig, which has been rusted, and dead for years. The old outhouse is "crappy" (completely full up).

The first drilling program here at the Victoria camp started with the outhouse, two shifts, and twenty-fours a day if necessary, as this was priority number one. No ceremonial ribbon cutting, just get the job done. Disregarding any preconceived notions about the Russian work ethic, the project was finished on time, under budget, and took only one shift. After drilling the hole, boards were ransacked from the previous outhouse and nailed into place to form the new and improved outhouse. After placing some boards over the poop hole, and not bothering to include a luxurious box seat to sit on, or a roof, the crew called it quits. According to their standards, this was good enough, at least for today. I hope that we won't freeze our butts off, as it is right out in the open. I'm sure if we had a bottle of vodka, we would have all sat down and had a toast to a job well done.

Back inside our living quarters, Peter approached Ray and I and motioned us to his bedside. Walking over to the doorway, he drew the blanket door closed, paused, and then cautiously looked around briefly, as if the *Russian Woodpecker project* was still in effect. Reaching under his bed, and with a slight grunt, he hauled the hernia-causing suitcase of his, onto the bed.

Ray looked over to me and grunted something. He thought briefly about getting his notebook to write stuff down, but changed his mind. Despite his thick glasses, I could tell his eyes were sparkling with anticipation. Despite my glasses, I'm sure he could tell mine were sparkling as well. Peter popped the locks. Humph. As if he couldn't trust us! Then he unveiled it to us. Gold and precious jewelry found in the form of food. Canned food! Spam, beef ravioli, beef stroganoff, chili con carne, salmon, chicken, you name it; a gourmet's delight. It was a feast for our eyes. We were comforted with the thought that, at least we wouldn't die for the *want* of a good selection of food to choose from, if Alex's meals became banal (or if Gypsy was suddenly no longer around to greet us). Up here, in no man's land, food, at least temporarily to us, was more precious than gold. There is no one here to barter with, and you need food to survive.

Peter's food was free for the taking. No more locks on it. As he closed the suitcase and dropped it, unlocked, back under his bed, I just hoped that he remembered to bring a can opener from home.

CHAPTER 14
TURN UP THE HEAT - IT'S COLD!

Saturday May 7
Day 11

It's cold! The wind is howling and our room is only +12C (54F) as the three of us lie here in our sleeping bags, my heavy parka covering me. My old, blue down-filled sleeping bag has empty air pockets in it and is lumpy where the feathers have clumped together. The only reason I brought it to Russia was its lightness and easiness to pack in a suitcase. Ray is currently going over notes on soil descriptions of frozen soils, while Peter is quietly reading. I just finished walloping my RadioShack computer chess three times this morning.

Last night for supper, we had our customary rations of soup and day old bread; this morning it was pancakes and jam, although out of the cook's sight, I supplemented my breakfast with a Nutribar and a granola bar. Our boss, Bob Forsythe, is supposed to fly in today from the Flox site, just across Baydaratskaya Bay, and update us on the drilling program.

1:26pm

The helicopter, surprisingly, arrived in this weather. Winds are quite fierce. The second drilling crew from Labytnangi arrived. No Bob on the helicopter.

They never tell us anything such as why Bob wasn't on the plane. The weather personnel do not have direct lines of communication with the helicopter pilots. Their two-way radios are limited in scope and distance, and often they make use of a third party as a relay between them, to send messages to each other.

The helicopter flies in roughly every three days, but that schedule can vary, as quite often they have other priorities. If we hear the helicopter flying in, it's all hands on deck, and everybody scrambles out of camp to greet and participate in the quick unloading or loading of supplies and equipment. It's much like what you see on the TV series MASH, where everybody runs to remove the patients as quickly as possible from the incoming helicopter. In our case, the patients come in the form of supplies, equipment, and mail. With the helicopter's engines still running, the process usually takes less than 10 minutes, and then the pilot is on his way to his next destination, perhaps another camp or drilling rig. If the pilot cannot land, usually because of other priorities or commitments, he will signal us by circling once over camp, and then head off, usually north, to his next stop. Then we assume he will try to make it the next day.

2:30pm

Wind still blowing fiercely. We had a good lunch of soup, stew, and two cucumber slices. Here is a brief description of our camp. The main weather station has a large entrance storage area where they have pails of ice that are constantly being heated. In our living quarters, we have a small stove where a pail is heated as well. Water is precious in terms of the effort to heat the ice and fetching it. There is a small kitchen about four feet by four feet and an eating area room about ten feet by twelve. With twenty-three people in camp, eating is a rather sombre occasion; little talking, you eat, then get out to let the next group of people eat as there is only room for about five or six people at the table. Alexander the cook tries his best and is polite. The weather operations center is small, about ten feet by ten feet; maybe two or three people operate it. There is a building for the diesel generator, which produces the electricity. There is one outlet to each room. There is an old (filled) outhouse and a new hole in the ground for the new one. In our living shack, there are two bedrooms, one at each end, and a small washing area, with a sink and diesel stove, in between. A pail of ice is constantly being heated on the stove.

There is an old drilling rig from a few years ago which has rusted over and missing parts. Our living quarters is about twenty yards from the eating build-ing [weather station] and seventy yards from the outhouse towards the bay (Baydaratskaya Bay). Ray took a temperature reading outside. It was only -4C, but with the wind blowing, it seemed much colder. We are experiencing the true North. With the wind like this, we may be here a while. Bye. It's time to get back to my western book.

8:02pm

Wind is up to blizzard conditions, close to a whiteout. You can't see more than ten or fifteen yards. I wouldn't advise going to the outhouse. We can still see the eating building though. It's quite close. I spent the whole day sleeping, reading, eating, or playing chess. Three wins and three losses so far this trip against the computer. Bye.

9:11pm

Wind still howling. Our heater/stove ran out of fuel and being refueled now. Temperature in room is now +4C, but must be below freezing. We can see our breath. We sleep fully clothed, sweaters, underwear, and the works (except for Mukluks). You sleep with your money belt and passport on you, although most of the men are trustworthy.

Actually, this last statement is overblown. The main reason I slept with everything on was so that I didn't forget where I put them. Besides, it isn't as if they are going to steal things and then escape from camp. There is nowhere to go. Everyone here is trustworthy; although I have to admit, I did have a lapse in judgment in my youth and stole something once.

It was at the Oliver Supervalu, at the age of seven, when my short life of crime began. It began with a chocolate bar. During this time, many major things changed in the world that affected me directly and adversely. I found out what the word "inflation" meant in the real world, and it hit me hard. Almost overnight, the price of a chocolate bar went from a nickel (five cents) to a dime (ten cents), a one hundred percent increase. I knew the numbers because, and Mrs. Hopkins would vouch for me if she were still alive today, I was good at arithmetic. I could now buy only one chocolate bar instead of two with that dime. I was devastated. But since mom was supplying the dough at the time, in the form of an allowance, I would simply ask for more. No problem.

But my mom, not unlike other moms who all seem to have ESP, stopped me cold before I could finish stuttering, in my shy ways, my demands.

"No way! Everything is more expensive these days! Do you think money grows on trees?"

Moms can be so mean at times. I slunk back. I had no adequate response. My vocabulary was only in its beginning stages, so I had no viable comeback for that one.

At the Supervalu checkout counter, I was behind my mom one day, with an *English Toffee* chocolate bar in one hand and a dime to pay for it in the other. There were no taxes back in those days, but I knew there wouldn't be any change given back either because of that dreaded word *inflation*. As mom paid for her groceries and was heading for the exit door, the cashier was distracted briefly by another woman. In my haste of seeing mom leave without me, and not wanting to be left behind, I quickly followed her out the door. Inside the car, sitting on the back seat, since mom had the groceries in the front, I looked down. In one hand, I had the *English Toffee*, and in the other, I had the dime from which I was supposed to pay for the chocolate bar. Horror of horrors! I had forgotten to pay for it. I had stolen a chocolate bar. Mom had already started the car and was driving out the parking lot, and I was too embarrassed to tell her. I left it at that and was totally quiet the rest of the way home. It wasn't until years later (at least seven, because I wanted to make sure that the *Statute of Limitations* had passed. I was good in my Law class in grade nine as well), that I had the courage to tell her, or anyone about that horrendous act I had committed. I don't think I got a spanking when I finally confessed. Probably the *Statute of Limitations* included spankings.

But eventually, I was able to make reparations for my crime of forgetfulness in my youth. In May 2016, the Oliver Supervalu closed its doors for good to make way for the new *No Frills* store. I had worked there for the past nine years part time in the produce department (I was able to work there since they never caught me, and thus, didn't have a criminal record). On the final day, I wanted to have the honor of buying the very last product sold there. I sat on the windowsill next to the last cashier, waiting, telling her not to close the till for its last time until I made the official last purchase in the store. When the cashier cleared the last customer, I bought, and paid for, a can of peas and carrots for thirty-seven cents (75% off) and the cash register shut down for its final time in its sixty-year history. I also took this moment to take a picture of the cashier, Terry Brogan the wife of owner Wally Brogan, and myself with the receipt in my hand. A few days later, Supervalu had a final auction for all of the freezers, fridges, shopping carts, and accessories of the store. At this time, I approached Terry and presented her with a wrapped gift. She opened it. Inside was a framed photograph of the picture I took of the three of us, including me holding the receipt of that last product sold and...an *English Toffee* chocolate bar. She already knew the story behind that since I had told her and Wally about that a while back. We all had a good laugh. I appeased my fifty-one year guilty conscience. Of course, I now had to pay ninety-nine-cents for the chocolate bar plus tax. In addition, it had shrunk in size compared to the original ten-cent bar. And there was no "mom" handing over the dough this time.

— * —

This evening, with our living quarters being so cold, the three of us decided to walk to the next building to the dining room for warmth where the entertainment center was. There was no television to watch, or radio to listen to; only people, to replace those material objects.

As we passed the small communications room, we saw the two weather men playing games on their computer, a contrast to the rest of camp with its primitive nature, but probably typical of what we'd be doing back home in our age of technology.

The dining room was empty, other than for Arthur and Mesha, one of the drillers. Mesha was in fine form as he was in the midst of an intense speech he was giving to Arthur. With arms gesticulating with heart-felt emotion, you couldn't say he wasn't passionate with his orations. Arthur tried, at times, to interject, but to no avail. Mesha had the floor, and he wasn't giving it up easily. He was taking full advantage of it. He was in top form with his story telling.

Upon seeing the three of us enter, and realizing quickly that his lone audience of one could be increased four-fold, Mesha motioned us, with exuberance, to sit down and join them. We sat down, and over the next few hours, with Arthur interpreting, Mesha captivated us with his Russian story telling. Philosophy, religion, sports, the Russian culture, his life stories, politics, the world's problems; no subject was off limits. He had solutions to all. He kept us captivated and at bay. We were fascinated with his passion as he relished his role as storyteller. He was in a groove. He was on a roll. Occasionally we managed to get in a tidbit or two about our thoughts on certain subjects, but for the most part, it was he, Mesha, who was the one who entertained us.

Later on, as the sun desperately tried to disappear over the horizon, but couldn't, the lights started to flicker, hinting to Mesha that it was time to refuel its power source, the diesel generator. At about this same time, the heaters were being affected as well. But Mesha couldn't be bothered, and neither could we. As we sat in darkness, slowly getting colder by the minute, Mesha continued triumphantly on, holding us hostage to his tales.

Eventually he ran out of stories, at least for the evening, and we took that short walk back to our quarters. Our souls had been completely entertained for the evening, much more than a television set could ever have done. As Peter, Ray, and I were walking out the building, I took one last look back to the dining room. The entertainment center was now gone.

CHAPTER 15
THE KODAK MOMENT

Sunday May 8
Day 12

The same old routine; 8:00am-breakfast, 2:00pm-lunch, 8:00pm-supper. Footnote: About four days ago, a Russian on a ski-doo fell off and broke his hip. He had to be evacuated via helicopter. The room temperature is now +5C. We sit around in full gear, including toques and sleeping bags, and read books, snooze or whatever. Drilling should start tomorrow morning. We are still all in good cheer, but everyone restless to get the drilling program going and completed.

Last evening after we got back to our room from Mesha's entertainment party, one of the drillers came over to our side of the shack with his chess set. With hand gesturing and the odd English phrase, he obviously wanted to know if anybody played chess. Since my RadioShack chess set was right in front of us on the table, I had to answer his call. And *that* was the beginning of a friendly, fun rivalry between Russia and Canada for bragging rights. I pulled out the tiny table from the corner of the room.

Andre, neatly groomed, clean-shaven with a mustache, of medium build with short brown hair, placed the chessboard on the tiny table and sat on the edge of Peter's bed. I pulled up the lone, dinky chair. We played three games. Although I concentrated and tried very hard at this Russian favourite pastime, of course I was no match. Three victories went to Andre. Andre, chess champion of the Arctic Circle! Of course, we were arrogantly dismissing any possible thought that there was anybody else playing chess at this moment inside the Arctic Circle. It was his glory for the day and I acknowledged that.

Upon reflection, I think it took a lot of courage on Andre's part to come over to our side of the shack and initiate a conversation with us with his limited Russian. It would have been easy for him to stay in his comfort zone and play chess with some of his comrades on their side. But by his initiative, he created an opportunity for two people on opposite sides of the world to come together, at least for a brief moment in time, and create a lifetime of memories (not to mention bragging rights).

This afternoon, Sunday, Ray and I decided to walk onto Baydaratskaya Bay, about 80 yards south of camp, to photograph ourselves with the Canadian flag. It was a nice, clear, windless day. We were still close to camp, so I don't think we created too much fuss about leaving its confines, especially relating to possible polar bears in the area.

Rummaging through the main storage area in the weather station, I found a stake to which I could attach my small flag that I had brought with me from home. I thought briefly about taking one of the stakes from the row that was planted on the bay just west of us, with its orange flagging and all, but somehow I don't think the drilling crew would have been too happy with me.

I tied the flag to it, and then, on a large piece of cardboard wrote:

Baydaratskaya Guba (Bay)

Arctic Circle

Lat. 69° Long. 68°

May 8, 1994

We then photographed ourselves individually holding the flag and sign. Taking off my large parka hood so that it wouldn't interfere with the picture, I took Ray's photo first, with him standing there, holding both the flag and sign. Then we reversed roles.

Prior to my photo op, I told Ray to remove his hood also so that it didn't interfere with the picture. But Ray was stubborn and left it on. He reassured me that he could see just fine, as he gazed through the viewfinder. I sat down on the ice, planted the Canadian flag proudly beside me in the snow and held the sign to my chest.

This was a proud moment for me. This was a photograph I would show my family and friends back home I was actually inside the Arctic Circle in Russia.

I would frame this and place it on my fireplace mantle next to the photographs of me on my next adventures of climbing Mount Everest and landing on the moon.

Ray snapped the picture.

Years later, I still quietly cuss and curse Ray every time I look at the photograph in my photo album, of my historic moment on this earth, that shows half of me and half the inside of Ray's parka hood. I also have a half and half photo of myself, and selfsame hood, holding the Canadian flag, standing in front of the newly completed outhouse.

It's like those three or four rare Kodak moments in life when you have a close encounter with an alien being, or see a UFO, and your camera mysteriously doesn't work. Of course, just because you happened to have a beer, or ten, at the time, the world doesn't believe you. Skeptical world! But this time it was the person behind the camera, i.e. *Ray Hunt*, who failed me. Ugh!

During this afternoon that *Ray Hunt* was showing me (and the world) that any aspirations of his of ever becoming a professional photographer were non-existent, we took time out to play with Gypsy. I also took a picture of her. She had followed us onto the ice, making sure we were using her escort services as we left camp. With a friendly and happy go lucky nature, she follows us everywhere. She sleeps in the large utility room in the weather station when her services are not required.

8:03pm

We did the same routine today. Wind has calmed down. It is -8C. We lit a couple of emergency candles as our room was down to +5C. Stove isn't giving off as much heat. We read in our full clothing and sleeping bags and parkas. We took photos of ourselves on the Baydaratskaya Bay with our Canadian flag. We played with the dog and seen a gull. The drillers practiced drilling a hole. Watched the Russians almost complete the outhouse. It doesn't take much to please me. Here I am, living in the Arctic Circle with our room at +5C, and I will be happy with a completed outhouse. Supper delayed for half an hour.

Monday May 9
Day 13

The boredom of camp is over. The drilling program has started with ten meters drilled today. Fourteen holes, previously surveyed and staked out, are approximately one hundred meters apart and run from the shoreline into the bay. These holes are in close proximity to where the proposed gas pipelines(s) will cross from the Yamal Peninsula onto the seabed of Baydaratskaya Bay and continue to the other side where Bob, John, Peter 2, and the second Russian drilling crew are at the Flox weather station. From there, the pipeline will connect to Europe to feed her energy needs. Later on, Bob was to come over to our site, and with his GPS unit, record the coordinates to confirm that the location of the drilling holes were correct.

At the hotel meeting a week or so ago, Bob prudently decided to start the first holes, both the Flox and Victoria sites, furthest out into the bay, and have the last ones drilled closer to shore. It would be safer. Even though the ice was still perhaps a half meter thick in places, enough to carry the weight of the drilling rig, it was starting to break up.

Earlier today, the first drilling crew went out with Peter to set up the drilling rig. The rig, along with a metal shack used as a shelter, was hauled out by a tractor-driven sledge to its first location. After piercing the ice, the auger continued through two or three meters of water before reaching the seabed, where, four or five meters were drilled and samples taken at various depths. After the soil was brought up, either by auger (disturbed samples) or Shelby tube extraction (undisturbed), the samples were analyzed and logged for soil descriptions, permafrost conditions (frozen), hole number, depth, and all that fun engineering stuff. Ray and Peter 1 are doing the logging here at the Victoria site, while John and Peter 2 are logging at the Flox site. My responsibilities, for the most part, are yet to come. I will be analyzing the laboratory and anything related to it. Here, my focus will be on notetaking on the methods of extraction, storage, and transportation of the soil samples. Once all this is done, the logs will be given to Bob, who will do a final report based on the observations of the two drilling programs.

The new toilet is now complete, although there is no seat, just a hole. You have to kind of do an awkward squat. Yesterday afternoon and evening, the room temperature constantly increased until it was a balmy +22C, about 72F. I guess it depends upon which way the wind is blowing Today has very little wind and is quite nice out, perhaps the nicest.

Evening meal delayed half an hour as the generator wasn't working. The temperature outside was not that cold, maybe 0C or perhaps not even freezing, but slight wind blowing made it cool. Our cabin is cozy tonight, +29C. I spent the whole day snoozing, reading or eating Nutribars, raisins, or granola bars, or collecting pails of snow for water. The drilling site is only about two and a half kilometers away, and you can see the flag markers from our cabin. Generator is back on. Sunset is from about 10:00pm and rises about 2:00am. However, since it is only slightly below the surface, it is quite light. You can see for a few kilometers. On this trip, I am now five wins and seven losses against the computer. It's time to challenge it again.

While the Russians collected ice for their buckets to heat for coffee, tea, etc., I was busy collecting snow. Obviously not as efficient, but what did I know. And I didn't have an axe with me, like they did. I was just trying to do something in camp that seemed useful.

Initially, the plans were for me to fly from the laboratory to a nearby city and have the weekend off. As so often is the case in Russia, most of the plans go by the wayside. The logistical aspect of this wouldn't have made any sense either. We were too far from any town. I stayed with the drilling crew until the drilling was done and then headed back to the laboratory. In the end, everything turned out much better for me in the long run.

To keep me entertained, I brought on this trip with me a deck of cards, bible tapes, and a radio, the latter of which was relatively useless up here since we couldn't pick up anything with clarity. As far as sleeping went, we generally slept fully clothed. I usually kept my fox-furred hooded parka close to me to keep my face and body cozy and warm.

At this point, there is virtually twenty-four hours of daylight.

Tuesday May 10
Day 14

Although the safety limit of seventy-two kilometers per hour wind velocity was not reached, the drilling crew didn't go out today due to the cold, -8C.

The safety issues Arthur talked about at the hotel in Labytnangi few days ago included some of the following details concerning the drilling program on the ice.

-Maximum twenty meters per second (seventy-two kilometers per hour) wind conditions allowed.

-Take at least two measurements of ice thickness; minimum ten centimeters (four inches).

-If ice movement is detected, don't go on it.

-Ice-cracks greater than five centimeters are the danger zone.

-Thirty-to-fifty meters marks good vision.

-Get permission from the main manager before starting work.

-Someone with a shotgun needs to be on site at all times.

-A radio is needed if you are more than four kilometers from base.

-Stay at least one and a half meters from the drilling rig and make sure exit paths are clear.

-Place flammable equipment in closed metal boxes.

Despite the wind, the helicopter, after stopping briefly at the Flox weather station, managed to land here and drop off some supplies. Mr. Famienko was on board, and after talking briefly to us, left ten minutes later.

Tonight, Andre came over, and I introduced him to my electronic chess game. I showed him the sixteen different levels of difficulty on it, and after selecting one of the more difficult ones, he, not surprisingly, won. Throughout this journey, I stayed at the middle level eight.

CHAPTER 16
CHESS CHAMPION OF THE ARCTIC CIRCLE!

Wednesday May 11
Day 15

Last night I skipped supper and this morning skipped breakfast as well, as I wasn't too hungry. Peter was in a grumpy mood today, so I tried to avoid him and stay out of his way. Earlier this morning he lost his toque down the poop hole in the outhouse. How on earth do you lose a toque down a toilet, or in this case, down a deep hole in the frozen earth? He must have taken at least one peek down and that was the end of it. No rescue attempts were ever made. It would have been futile and gut retching.

Centuries from today, archaeologists, due to the "so-called" global warming, will unearth this toque and probably spend countless, wasted hours trying to find its victim, who might be buried nearby. Then they, from this lone extraction, with its Dutch label still attached to it, and with their creative minds, will come up with some exotic theory about how the Dutch were the first ones to inhabit this otherwise, inhospitable land during this era. Or perhaps they will find the remains of this book first and have the mystery solved, thus saving themselves much time and effort (and creative thought).

This afternoon was bright and sunny with no clouds or wind, so I took a walk around the perimeter of the camp. I wore my sunglasses, one of our prerequisites for this trip, to prevent the sun's glare from reflecting off the snow and possibly causing snow blindness. Unfortunately, none of the Russians has them as they are too expensive, or perhaps simply don't have access to them.

This evening, I was called into the weather monitoring room to check out the laboratory shear vane apparatus. This simple device gives the quick, undrained shear strength of the soil sample. Part of my job is to become familiar with what laboratory equipment they have, both on and off site, photograph, and include this information in my report.

Later, Andre and I had our traditional evening chess match. It was a historic night for me, May 11, 1994, as I was crowned, for the first time, as chess champion of the Arctic Circle! After losing the first game, I won the next two, although there were times it seemed that Andre was getting bored and not paying attention since I took a long time between moves. Not that this was my strategy, as some chess players use, it's just that I like to take my time (in other words, I was slow).

Speaking of championships, there once was a rumor circulating around that I was ping pong champion of Oliver, British Columbia, my hometown. But that rumor is false. It was spread by someone trying to impress his girlfriend at the time. But now I can celebrate (and brag) about something that isn't rumor, but fact. I am the chess champion of the Arctic Circle...at least for the day...unofficially of course!

Thursday May 12
Day 16

Since my job involves not only laboratory observations, but observations of sample handling, storage, and transportation methods to and from the site as well, I spent the day shift with *toqueless Pete* and the drilling crew.

This morning, I walked alongside the tractor-driven sledge and shelter, with everyone else, as it made its way slowly to the site two and a half kilometers away. Each day, this routine is repeated, with the tractor and shelter returning to camp in the evening. Gypsy was always amongst the group, cheerful and excited as usual, barking out her morning greetings to everyone. It was a cheerful, bright, sunny day, -3C and no wind, and the forty-minute walk was refreshing. It was nice to get out of camp for a change. Since Ray had done the previous shift, Peter was the drilling observer for today, as they alternate each day.

Once everything was set up and drilling got started, I stayed back, out of everyone's way and monitored their progress. Actually, I wasn't really monitoring, since I'm not an expert on drilling, I was more or less learning how everything was done.

With the relatively shallow depths that the holes were drilled, there weren't many extensions needed, and going through mostly silts and sands, drilling went smoothly. At certain intervals, soil samples were brought up for Peter to do visuals on, and log. Occasional samples that contained ice lensing were extracted from the seabed using a Shelby tube attached to the end of the drilling rig. A Shelby tube is a simple steel tube, about three inches in diameter and twelve to eighteen inches in length and is pushed vertically (down) into the soil, thus bringing up an undisturbed sample, which keeps its stratification and lensing (if there is any) intact.

I kept a record of how the frozen samples were kept frozen at the drill site, how unfrozen samples were kept unfrozen, where they were stored, record temperatures inside the shelters as well as temperatures outside, transportation methods back to the weather station, where they were kept, what their final destination was, and how they were transported there.

Obviously, as part of our required "job list" of items, we brought thermometers like those used to test concrete when it's being poured. We used these each day to determine temperatures, including the temperatures in our room where we slept, since there was so much variation in it, and sometimes we could see our breath (not that our room temperature readings were incorporated in our report; we were just curious). Sometimes, if ice lenses were difficult to see, the thermometer was inserted into the soil to determine if it was frozen. After the sample was labeled (hole number, depth, site, etc.), it was stored temporarily during the day in the shelter, or left outside in an insulated box, depending upon whether it was unfrozen or frozen. Later on, as the drilling program was winding down and the weather turned milder, getting above freezing, it became a challenge to keep the samples from thawing; but we managed.

The portable shelter, about the size of a large shed, approximately ten feet by ten feet, remained seated on the sledge as it was driven back and forth each day from camp to the hole locations on the ice. Upon reflection, I suppose the shed was brought back each day for two reasons; one, in case of thawing, we didn't want to find it the next day broken through the ice and resting on the bottom of the bay, and number two, to have shelter, as we travelled back and forth, against an intruding polar bear.

The soil samples, once properly labeled, would then be placed in insulated boxes and transported by helicopter to the laboratory back in Obskaya. There, they would undergo further analysis and testing such as thaw settlement and triaxial strength tests, or be rerouted by cargo plane to Moscow for more sophisticated testing. So, if I seemed to imply that, up to this point, I wasn't doing much during my time spent at Victoria station that really wasn't the case. I was recording pertinent information needed and also developing the overall outline for my report. I was gleaning information off Peter and Ray when they came in after their shifts and making notes.

For the next ten and a half hours, the drilling crew did the drilling while Peter examined and logged the soil samples. Gypsy, having done her official greetings to everyone that morning, sat quietly on a blanket next to the shelter, content, while I did my observations and note taking. At the lunch and coffee breaks, we made tea in the warm shack and had sandwiches.

After finishing hole numbers 4, 5 & 6, we were finished for the day. Alongside the tractor sledge, as it chugged slowly along, we made the nice, relaxing walk back to camp. With the sun still shining brightly, and with Gypsy proudly in the lead, the main goal now, both hers and ours, was supper. Overall, it was a very pleasant and satisfying day.

At supper, Ray took one look at his supper and remarked, "Where's the dog (Gypsy)?"

I defended the world chess championship of the Arctic. After getting clobbered the first game, Andre gave me a stalemate the second game even though he had me. The third game I won, although it was more of a giveaway. My record is three wins, five losses, and one tie against Andre.

Friday May 13
Day 17

Today, after being in camp for one week, I was bored, so I decided to spend the next twenty-four hours completely redecorating our sleeping quarters and changing things around. I started with squeaky. I slightly shifted the front of it a couple of feet so I now slept at a slight angle, rather than parallel, to the central table, thus giving us more room. Then, I placed my small Canadian flag centrally on the clothesline strung diagonally across the room holding our assortment of laundry. Although we weren't all Canadian, this would be the center piece to the new look of the room. Satisfied, although no appreciation was given by the "other two" in the room, other than a couple of grunts (as they were too busy reading), I spent the next twenty-three hours and fifty-eight minutes of the day lying on squeaky, looking up at the flag, in self appreciation of a job well done.

We have completed five out of fourteen holes that we have to do. Talked to Bob and John on the CB, but the reception was poor. Bob will fly here on Monday. The helicopter landed here today. Mr. Famienko visited briefly for about ten minutes. A few Russians from here left. Used our bread from Labytnangi (which is heavy and hard as a rock) as weights in my exercises tonight.

Saturday May 14
Day 18

Lost four times to the computer today, although all were very good games. Walked around the camp and listened to bible tapes. There are seven holes left to go.

One thing that never dawned on me, while I was in camp, was the fact there was no liquor here. I'm not sure why. We never had any, nor seemed to miss it. I don't know if there were strict rules prohibiting it because they didn't want people drunk wandering around camp or working, or because they didn't feel it necessary to include in their supply inventory (unless of course, the Russians were keeping the vodka to themselves). Either way, obviously, we never saw anyone drunk, and all the Russians were well behaved throughout the time spent here.

Sunday May 15
Day 19

The reign is over. Losing four of six games of chess to Andre this evening, he is the new champion. I reigned for a total of four days, the shortest length of time in the history of chess tournaments. But then again, after thinking about it, I guess Andre's first reign was shorter, only three days in length. Little consolation in that though. With my limited abilities, I may never get another chance to be king.

As we competed, Ray read a book (or wrote little things in the notebook/diary of his), while Arthur and Peter sat on Peter's bed, in deep discussion, defending their philosophical viewpoints about country, politics, religion, and solving the world's food problems.

Monday May 16
Day 20

The Dynamic Cone Penetration test, or DCP, is a simple test where a pointed steel rod, mounted on a small rig, is hammered into the ground by mechanical force. There are markings on the rig and rod that allows the worker to measure distance the cone travels with each blow. By counting and recording the number of blows per foot travelled, the soil density and its properties can roughly be determined; the greater the number, the denser the soil. A gravel type of soil will give a high blow count, while a silt or clay will give a low count; unless, of course, you hit a rock, which screws up everything. But that is usually self-evident and noted.

But before you do this test, you must *first* be able to start the rig. Today was an exasperating day as I went out with the DCP crew of Arthur and Mesha (Michael) to do testing near the holes. Everyone else was in camp since they were changing to evening shifts. Until now, only one twelve hour shift per day was done. It took two hours for the cone to hit sea bottom hardness (10.2m), then two more hours to start the stupid machine. Apparently, it has been a piece of crap since day one.

I stood there watching them, alternating from one foot to the other and shivering, not really from cold, but more from boredom. As I watched them helplessly, my mind wandered, and I couldn't help but think perhaps we might see a polar bear or two. This would perk things up a bit and we would see Mesha with his shotgun in action. After all, you can only stand boredom for so long. I scanned the horizon far and wide in vain, but typical of my boring life, I didn't see any. I was out of luck. As I paced back and forth, my mind wandered again.

I remembered the story once told to me, not sure by whom or if it's true, about the Russians (or maybe the Eskimos), how they trapped a polar bear. With a long, sharp ice pick, they would chip away a large hole in the ice, perhaps ten feet deep (they had lots of ice back then in those days before the so-called "global warming"). Then they would fill the hole with ashes from their campfire (they had large campfires with an abundance of trees back then too). They followed this by lining the perimeter of the hole with dried peas that were harvested from their summer gardens (they had long summers also back then). Then, they would hide behind a snowbank and wait. When the polar bear came to take a pea, they would kick him in the ash hole.

...With the sound of the thousandth attempt to try and start the DCP machine, I was brought back to my senses. We didn't bring our ice picking tool with us, so the idea of trapping a polar bear was out of the question. But I did have to take a pee.

It was a beautiful day today of about 0C, or actually thawing...The ice is creaking and groaning and there are numerous cracks and upheavals. The helicopter came three times, but Bob didn't arrive. We have splurged into Peter's kitchen the last two days since we are getting tired of the same-old Russian food. I had Chili con Carne today and coffee, and last night, Beef Stroganoff. I spent most of the time today taking pictures, or wandering around out on the bay. Footnote: 5:30pm. Each of the last few evenings, Bob has phoned over the CB to update us.

CHAPTER 17
FORBIDDEN TERRITORY

Tuesday May 17
Day 21

The drillers were out on Baydaratskaya Bay and the camp was fairly empty. Drilling now was much closer to camp, as each day's drilling brought them closer to the shoreline. Spring was fast approaching, and the ice was thawing with severe upheavals, sometimes three feet high. But work continued, as it was still considered safe to finish the job.

The long abandoned skeletal remains of the old weather station three kilometers north of camp were off limits. No one without the armed escort of someone with a shotgun was allowed to leave the camp perimeters because of polar bears in the region. And yet, it beckoned me.

It was there within sight of camp, although far off in the distance, with its homely appearance, vainly trying to maintain a lonely existence against the bitter elements that the whitewashed world around it presented.

We were reaching the end of our term here and in another day or so, would be packing our things and flown, by helicopter, back to Labytnangi. The Russians would be flown elsewhere to get their next meal ticket.

The day was pleasant, 0C, with clear blue skies, sunny, and little possibility of a storm suddenly arising. Visibility was good, and you could see the distant broken structure with the naked eye. The frozen tundra in between, was thawing slightly and had a gentle layer of perhaps six inches of snow on it. The terrain was flat. I was bored and restless. I decided to chance it.

I left camp undetected, since no one was around except for the few non-related drilling personnel, and headed north. It took me about half an hour to reach the destination with no problems whatsoever and had a quick look around. Not really much to see. As expected, just an odd assortment of vertical steel pipes still standing in the ground with some scattered on the ground loosely. That was it. Not much more than what I had already seen from camp. But, at least it was nice to go for a walk, get out of camp, and have a bit of freedom. I stayed only for about ten minutes, and then headed back.

I was confident as I walked along, unhurried, occasionally looking over my shoulder for the remote possibility of polar bears, but none were seen. About halfway back, it slowly dawned on me that perhaps this idea of a nature walk wasn't exactly the brightest of ideas after all. I hadn't told anyone about my plans, and if something went wrong, they would have no idea where to start looking for me. I could have been a polar bear's lunch, or slipped on the ice and sprained my ankle, or had some other health issue. It would have been a struggle to make it back on my own. I managed to remain calm, although anxiety was now starting to creep in. I started to get goosebumps. It's like that feeling you get when walking down a dark alley at night, alone (of course, why do you put yourself in this situation in the first place, idiot! Criticism of myself only, as I realize some people don't have a choice), far from home, striving to stay calm; then, when you near home, your imagination runs wild with thoughts of bad guys lurking in the shadows about to pounce on you. Then it's an all-out run to home, hoping you don't fumble and drop your keys in the process.

I increased the number of "look over the shoulders" (LOTS) watching for, and expecting, a polar bear to suddenly spring forth from its camouflaged six inch snow cover, charging with glee for his or her free meal. But I made it back safely to camp, without any mishap, in time for *my* free meal. As I entered the camp's perimeter, one of the Russians saw me, perhaps the cook's assistant, I'm not sure, but he didn't say anything to me, nor to anyone else as far as I know. Nobody ever said anything to me afterwards, and I never told anyone. I knew I would get a good lecture and scolding if they ever did find out.

At the time, I didn't really think too much about my walk in forbidden territory. It was routine, not really much chance of encountering a polar bear. It is only years later, when I look back on this incident, I realize the potential dangers I might have encountered, and how stupid I was. It wasn't worth it. Even though I brought my camera with me, I hadn't even bothered taking it out of the case to take a picture. There was nothing worthwhile to take a picture of. It was just an empty site with pipes scattered, abandoned, unwanted, something nobody really cared about anymore.

What was it that drew me to this place to the point of perhaps risking my life for something so futile? Was it boredom that caused me to leave camp against all common sense, throwing caution to the wind as they say? Was it curiosity and disregard to authority, perhaps like the biblical story of the Garden of Eden, where you're told not to do something, but go ahead and do it anyways? At that time in my life, I was relatively young, thirty-five years of age, and, as they say, "Invincible." Sometimes we do things against all logic.

I remember one time when I was a young teenager helping my dad shingle our new barn roof. I was bored so I played a game with myself. I looked towards the other end of the roof and thought, "If I close my eyes and walk towards it, I wonder how close I can get to the edge and stop, without falling over?" Therefore, I closed my eyes, took about ten steps, and then stopped. I opened my eyes. I was about three feet from the edge. Then it dawned on me. How stupid can I be? If I had taken two more steps, I would have fallen over the edge and hurt myself severely, or at least emotionally, since there was a huge pile of cow manure right below it. It never dawned on me that I might continue *too far* and fall over. It's amazing how dumb we are when we are teenagers. But then again, perhaps it's only me.

I think that despite our (my) youthful stupidity, God has protected us, much more than we realize or appreciate, from the dangers that are always present in our lives. I give thanks for that.

But having said all this, the question arises. If I had the chance to do it all again, would I have done it? Have I learned from that experience?

With the "shingling the roof" experience, I probably would have repeated my mistake since that was simply a case of stupidity and not realizing the consequences; and I would have ended up saying "hello" to the manure pile.

As for the trip to the forbidden territory, I'm not sure. In a spiritual sense, we are given an innate *wanting* to seek out the purpose of life; God, universe, planet, etc. In this case, all I was seeking out was the purpose of a few metal pipes sticking out from the ground. I was young and healthy, it was a clear, sunny day with no bad weather conditions, and visibility was good for kilometers.

The snow level was too low for a polar bear to hide behind (unless he was a very tiny bear), and boredom (or cabin fever) was setting in. Being a Christian, I felt I was in God's protection. But then again, God reminds us not to tempt him. We can't expect him to get us out of every jam we put ourselves into.

Was it blind faith? Or was I tempting God?

CHAPTER 18
MODERN TECHNOLOGY, GPS, AND SATELLITE PHONES

Despite its bulkiness, the satellite phone we had was considered a godsend. Just power it up and you could connect virtually to anywhere in the world. Of course, it was extremely expensive to use, amounting to at least a few dollars per minute, so the calls we made were kept short. But as time goes on, the technology improves; the phones get lighter, costs become cheaper, more satellites come into operation, and thus, coverage improves.

As a Canadian, I am very proud to know that research has proven that Canada is the world's leader when it comes to telecommunications.

A few years ago, a British archaeology expedition was digging and unearthing artifacts in an ancient city when, at the ten foot depth, they found copper wire. It shouldn't have been there, considering the time period. Thus, they concluded Britain had telecommunications over one hundred and fifty years ago.

A few months later, the Americans were digging at an archaeological site in United States and found copper wire at the thirty foot depth, which shouldn't have been there for that time period. They concluded that United States had telecommunications over *two hundred* years ago.

When the Newfies, short for Newfoundlanders, the politically incorrect butt of all Canadian jokes, decided to do some digging of their own in their own back yard, they dug down fifty feet. Guess what they found? No, you're wrong. They didn't find anything. They found absolutely nothing. The Newfies then made the conclusion that Canadians, but especially Newfoundlanders, were the first ones three hundred years ago to invent...*wireless technology!*

It's amazing how logic works!

Tuesday (cont.)
Day 21

In the late afternoon, our boss Bob Forsythe flew in by helicopter from the Flox station thirty kilometers away, across the bay. He was here to update us on the overall progress so far and needed to do some GPS (Global Positioning System) surveys on the holes here to confirm they were drilled in the proper places. I volunteered to walk the two and a half kilometer line with him. Surprisingly, we weren't escorted by anyone with a shotgun. I suppose Mesha was just too tuckered out to walk another five kilometers before supper.

Even Gypsy wasn't too enthused to go out either, and barely did her greeting duties to Bob, before retreating back to the comforts of her blanket at the weather station.

As Bob set up the hand-held apparatus for each hole, I suggested that, not only should he record the longitude and latitude of each hole, but also, the number of satellites that he managed to latch on to. The device shows the number of satellites it connects with that happen to be flying over at the time. Sometimes the satellite coverage can be spotty and takes a few minutes to have one fly over. It there was a discrepancy of readings between the holes, we could assume the hole that had more satellite connections would be more accurate.

We started with the furthest hole, then worked our way back. After my long walk this morning, I was extremely tired when we finished and came back to camp. My legs and thighs were starting to cramp up. I was not used to all this walking after sitting around for so long in camp.

After supper, Bob got out the portable (if you can call it portable) satellite phone, and with Ray, Peter, and I tagging along, walked outside the w. s. to a clearing near the outhouse. We were then each given the opportunity to phone home to North America, or in Peter's case, Holland.

The phone, and its accessories, was the size of a suitcase and weighed about forty pounds. After setting it up and waiting a few minutes for a satellite to fly over, Bob made the first call to his family. With satellite phone technology being fairly new and in its infancy at this time, at least to the average person, this was quite impressive to me.

After Bob finished his call, he showed us how to use it. He politely asked us to keep our calls short, as satellite phone calls were extremely expensive.

When it came to my turn, I followed Bob's instructions and dialed the twelve, or perhaps closer to a google of numbers, whatever it took, to make the overseas call to my parent's place back in Oliver, British Columbia.

Here I was, outside, standing on a patch of snow-covered frozen tundra in Siberia, just inside the Arctic Circle, phoning home, wireless, to North America. The wonders of technology! Mom and dad, but especially mom, would be highly impressed with me phoning her from where I stood.

With almost twenty-four hours of daylight here at this time, the evening was a beautiful setting when I made my phone call. It would be almost noon back in Oliver.

I heard the sound of the phone ringing. Wow. Cool! I had managed to latch onto at least one satellite in orbit overhead. After a few short rings, mom answered.

"Hello?"

"Hi mom, it's Larry."

"Who?"

I guess the reception was a bit poor, or mom had forgotten that she had a son named Larry, so I changed my position, walked a few yards and adjusted my torso 180 degrees.

"It's Larry, how's it going?"

"Oh, hi Larry, it's going good. Dick (my dad) is just outside mowing the lawn."

"Great. I'm phoning from just outside a remote weather station in northern Russia. I am here just inside the Arctic Circle. It's pretty neat. I am standing outside on the frozen ground as I speak. We arrived just a few days ago by helicopter." I was excited as I told her of my adventures. I was sure that she was excited to hear from me, after not calling her for so long.

"That's nice," was her simple, quiet response. Silence...pause. Hmm, well, maybe she wasn't quite as excited as I thought she would be. But as I continued on, telling her about life in camp and my adventures, she interrupted me.

"Hang on Larry, the soups boiling. I have to take it off the stove...Long, long silence. After a $15.00 long distance satellite phone bill for the thirty seconds of silence that followed, mom was back on the line.

"Hi Larry, I just turned off the stove. We're having carrot soup for lunch today. Now what were you talking about?"

At this point I decided to cut the conversation short. I passed on my greetings and well wishes to everyone, and I said goodbye.

I'm sure that on my next adventure of scaling Mount Everest and then becoming an astronaut, having just landed on the moon, that when I phone mom from its lunar surface, mom's first response will be, "Hang on Larry, the soups boiling. I have to take it off the stove. We're having carrot soup for lunch today."

CHAPTER 19
SAYING GOODBYE TO CAMP VICTORIA

Wednesday May 18
Day 22

This morning the three of us welcomed a guest to join us at the breakfast table, Bob. Breakfast was on us, as we graciously allowed him to sample from our fine, rarely changed, menu of porridge, bread, and tea. I never did ask him how food was at the Flox station, and he never volunteered any comparisons to our meal either.

I'm not sure where he slept last night. There was no room for that big frame of his in our room. If he tried, his feet would have been dangling out into the hallway, and we would be tripping over him every time we made our three or four times a night, pee. I don't think the Russian drillers across from us would have accepted him either. There was no room there as well. He probably slept at the weather station with the weather personnel, or with Gypsy in the storage room.

At the breakfast table, Bob, after talking with Jim Oswell last night on the satellite phone, confirmed to us that a helicopter was coming today to pick us up and fly us out to Labytnangi. Our drilling program finished last night with all fourteen holes completed.

Since the helicopter could arrive at any moment, we gathered our things and packed our suitcases quickly. We didn't need an SOS card for Peter's suitcase now, since it was much lighter with the depletion of most of its contents with the help of his two fellow rats in the room. My medium sized carry-on was extending its rip, with all the books it held.

To save weight, all my suitcases were of the lightweight, cloth variety, in stark contrast to the olden days gone by with their heavy, metal trunks, which the early settlers brought with them from overseas. Until recently, my mom still had an old, blue metal trunk that her parents had brought with them from Austria at the turn of the century. But when she was moved into an old folk's home in 2017, we had to sell the house, so the trunk ended up going to Janet and John West, with their garage of antiques in Penticton. I squeezed the air out of my patchy sleeping bag and squeezed it into my lightweight suitcase.

One of the last things to take care of was my Canadian flag. Perhaps, to show the world I actually was inside the Arctic Circle, and as part tradition of all early explorers, I looked for a place for its final resting place.

With the flag hidden in my outer parka pocket, I wandered through camp. The top of the outhouse was one possibility, but that was too obvious, and would have been seen quickly and possibly uprooted by some patriotic Russian going to the bathroom. Finding no other place suitable in camp, I considered the old structure eighty yards north of camp, with its abandoned, still standing pipes. It seemed to be a good choice, and nobody would notice it right away. I walked over there, found an upright metal pipe, and with a piece of string, tied the Canadian flag. Despite the great friendships I made here in Russia, as a proud Canadian, it was still nice to have a moment of patriotism to the country where I was born. Should I salute it? No, that was too sappy. Get real.

I am reminded of the time when, in Oliver in 2017, I was replacing my torn and weather-beaten Canadian flag that stood on a flagpole in my garden, next to the roses. My neighbour Jessica, and a couple of her friends, were working outside on their car, paying no attention to me. But once I had the old flag taken down and the new one in place and hoisted, I suddenly heard singing. There, standing proudly, hand over his heart, Jessica's friend was singing our national anthem "Oh Canada," while his wife looked on in amusement. Not to feel left out and unpatriotic, I also placed my hand over my heart, but didn't attempt to sing, considering my lack of musical talent. He actually sang the whole national anthem. I was impressed. We all laughed when he had finished. It was an icebreaker, and since I didn't know them that well, it was a good opportunity for me to say hello to them and be acquainted.

A few weeks later, my sisters and I had to sell my mom's house. Because of the connections I made with my neighbour at the flag raising ceremonies, I decided to donate much unwanted furniture to Jessica. The tears of joy she had, when she came over to look at the furniture, were amazing. She and her children were not well off financially, and were going through a rough time. The furniture was a treasure trove. That evening, a convoy of their friends, relatives, children, cats, dogs, all came marching down the street to my house, to help her load the furniture she wanted. Her sister, also in need, took a few things as well. The furniture that we considered as excess, and perhaps headed to the garbage dump, was a treasure chest for her sister. It's funny how God works. One open door leads to another. By that simple flag raising ceremony, I met some wonderful people and made new friends. In the process, Jessica, her children, and her sister were gifted with greatly appreciated furniture.

I have since moved, and so have Jessica and her children. I still see her occasionally, working at the gas station at her new job as cashier. She has a new place now, and I hope things continue to improve for her and her family.

— * —

Back to my flag raising here in Russia, I finished stringing it up. A slight breeze allowed the flag to flutter gently and gracefully. But, in my haste of not wanting to be seen by others, and worried that the helicopter might come at any time, I accidently placed it upside down! I was the one in distress, not my country. Ugh!

But I took it all in stride. My intentions were good. I left it as it was. I snapped a picture of it, upside down and all, fluttering hopelessly in the breeze. As I look back at this humorous moment, I am curious to know how long it actually lasted, or if it's still there today. Whether the Russians tore it down, or it succumbed to the ravages of the cold Arctic winds, I don't know and will never know. But the flag, at least for a moment in time, was on proud display, albeit upside down, showing that camp Victoria was once a home to proud Canadians.

— * —

Back at the sleeping quarters, I meet up with Peter and Ray, and we head to the dining room to thank Alex the cook for the meals he made for us during our time here. He did a fine job, all things considering, having to feed twenty-three people in camp. It wasn't easy, especially when you have only one helper and a limited variety of food to choose from. We head back to our sleeping quarters to wait for the sound of the distant helicopter telling us it's time to depart.

I lie down one last time on the squeaky cot, with its dirty, thin mattress, that has become squeakier and dirtier since I first arrived. I bring out my Louis L'Amour *Comstock Lode* book that has so faithfully provided me with my sole reading source for this trip. Peter decides to take a snooze while Ray, as usual, hunches over on the edge of his bed, writing little things down in his diary. I never did compare diaries with him. That would have been so much fun to do to see how he felt and thought throughout our journey.

Not much is being said. We are all in our own little worlds. I never really talked too much to Peter throughout our trip in Russia. He, for the most part up until the separation with the camps, usually hung out with Peter 2. I think we were more interested about the Russians and about their lifestyle. Also, we were more focused on adapting to whatever lay ahead in our adventures.

As I try to read my western, I am quietly nervous, but excited in anticipation of the things that are to come. At the same time, I am reflective of my life here in camp the past two weeks and of the friendships I have made. Being in camp amongst the Russians was an amazing experience.

I reminisce of the friendly chess challenges I had with Andre, in the little ten-foot by twelve-foot area of our side of the shack, while Ray sat on his bed reading, and Peter and Arthur sat on Peter's bed, having their philosophical discussions about the world around them. Also, being crowned unofficially, at least for a few days, as the chess champion of the Arctic Circle, that was pretty cool!

Or the evenings we spent in the dining room, entertained with Mesha's story telling, keeping us entranced, heating the room with his passion, while the outside temperatures grew colder.

I recall the times when Mesha forgot (or was too lazy) to refill the diesel tank that fed our heater that kept us warm. We simply put on an extra sweater or pulled our parkas over us, as we lay in bed, watching our breath as frost set in; no one ambitious enough to get up, go next door, and tell him, "We're cold, we need heat!" We couldn't be bothered.

The memories of the quaint characteristics of the shack, with its dirty, tiny washing area, and washing up in cold water from the cherry pail with its cool, handmade, pop-up spigot. And the three or four times a night I had to pee, putting on my parka, stepping onto the oil drum step, hoping that in my sleepy haze I didn't trip and fall into the snow drift, unzipping three layers of clothing, then writing my name in yellow in the snow; all good memories.

I will even miss the meals that Alex prepared for us each day. Although boring and very basic, it was food. What can I say? He tried his best. He was kept on his toes, as, at each mealtime, the men would line up against the dining room wall impatiently waiting their turn, glaring at, and putting pressure on, those eating at the table to "hurry up." Yet, quite often, Alex would give Peter, Ray, and I first seating, despite being at the end of the line. By the expressions on the Russian faces, they weren't all too happy about that, but they didn't say anything other than grumble quietly amongst themselves. But these were fun times, and what's a few squabbles between our comrades and us.

And if we didn't like the food, there was always Peter's food suitcase. But we always did our best to be courteous and polite and never complain; at least not until we were out of hearing distance of the cook, although Ray once slipped up with those infamous words at the dinner table, "Where's the dog?" Faux pas.

And speaking of Gypsy, I think of all the great times I had, playing with her. The dog, whose history was unknown, who faithfully greeted us each morning, proudly leading the drillers to the drilling sites each day, followed by the day ending journey back to camp, knowing that supper was waiting.

Then there's the outhouse. Despite the drilling program being a start to one of Russia's most ambitious energy projects in their history, involving the building of massive gas pipelines to Europe, the first hole drilled here... was for the outhouse. And it was built on time and under budget to boot! And Gypsy's escort services, although available, were never called upon, as the blizzards we faced weren't harsh enough (or we were too chicken to go to the bathroom when they were bad). And, I laugh when I think about the time when Peter lost his toque down the hole that one morning, and the look on his face when he came back from his trip, fuming...without his toque. Priceless!

I think about that one afternoon we had on the bay, as Ray and I photographed ourselves on the ice, posing with the Canadian flag. The happy spirits we had in pretense that we had just conquered something major like the North Pole, even though it was only the Arctic Circle, and then coming home, developing the pictures, and finding out we captured a picture of half of Ray's parka. Ugh!

Then, there was the time of frustration when I was with Arthur and Mesha, standing there for hours, as Mesha tried to start the stupid DCP machine.

And the proud moment I had of hoisting the Canadian flag, only to find out, too late, that I hung it upside down.

Finally, how can I forget that forbidden walk I took into no man's land, outside camp, where I tempted fate, or possibly, God.

Now, as I sit here waiting, I know I will always cherish these precious memories from the past two weeks I had, living at the Victoria weather station on Baydaratskaya Bay.

— * —

The distant, unmistakable sound of the helicopter wakes me from my thoughts. We scramble off our beds and pack our books, and anything else left, into our suitcases. Dragging them out the shack, I take one last look back, remembering the good moments I had in it, then head out to the landing site a few yards west of the w. s.

Most of our goodbyes have already been said to the few remaining stragglers left in camp. Some had left last night. Arthur and Bob, along with a few of the Russians, are quickly assembling their stuff and heading to the landing site as well.

Gypsy, with her patriotic duties as official greeter and send off representative of the camp, makes this one last walk together with us, tail wagging, excited, tongue hanging out, not quite knowing what is happening, but nonetheless, all an adventure to her. With our suitcases now splayed out in front of us at the landing site, each of us takes a moment to bend down and give her one last cheerful snuggle and say our goodbyes to her. She laps up the attention.

The Russian Sikorsky helicopter is now in full view. It approaches us slowly from the west, low, over the bay, the distinct sounds of the *whomp, whomp, whomp* of its massive rotor and blades being carried to us by the light wind.

Whether it's the sounds of a jet aircraft revving its engines to full throttle, with brakes on, ready for that final clearance from traffic control to take off, or the sounds of a distant helicopter, both, stir my senses to the fullest. They are special sounds to me. I come alive!

This is an exciting moment for me. This helicopter represents the next new chapter in my life, another adventure on this trip. Who knows where it will be taking me, or the places I go, or the people I meet.

The helicopter flies lower, perhaps now at fifty meters in elevation, as it heads towards us. I can see the pilot clearly through the plastic orb as he navigates this complex flying machine into position. He continues past us, to the weather station just a few yards behind us. He makes a slow circle above it, and then, without stopping, heads north. There is a pause as no one speaks. Utter silence comes over us. We don't know what to say. We are stunned! Even Gypsy is dumbfounded, as her previously wagging tail goes limp and is lowered to half-mast, as if to say, "What the f---?"

As we continue standing there, watching the helicopter, now far off in the distance, reality sets in and we all realize we are here for at least another day. Hmpff!

At this point, all the romantic, sentimental thoughts I had earlier this morning are gone. Crap! Back to the same old, crappy camp food and daily grind with all these grizzled characters we have to live with. And another night on that dirty, squeaky cot and dirty mattress that I thought I would never get rid of.

We wearily drag our suitcases back to our much-dreaded sleeping quarters. Gypsy, now far ahead of us, is no longer interested in us, or in our affections towards her. She is casually sniffing out anything in the snowdrifts, anything that might be of interest to her and distract her away from us. Perhaps she too, in that doggie mind of hers, had, for a moment, confident expectations that we would be gone, out of her hair, or in this case, her fur.

CHAPTER 20
TARGET PRACTICE

Wednesday (cont.)
Day 22

It is now lunchtime, and we are back in the dining room, eating our rations that Alex has doled out for us. After dumping our luggage unceremoniously back in the bedroom, a general letdown comes over us. The adrenaline rush of anticipation from a few moments ago, has worn off.

As we slurp our soup and chew our bread in silence, the dreary, almost humorous looks on our unshaven, grizzled faces says it all, so I take a moment to snap a picture of our group, alongside one other unnamed Russian, eating at the table with us.

So often in movies, you see a character, whom you love to hate, just given a new job opportunity of a lifetime and proceeds to tell his old, hated boss to shove it; only to find out later, he doesn't get his coveted job, and now has to plead to get his old job back. I'm glad we weren't like that, and harsh on Alex concerning the meals; otherwise we would be outside with Gypsy, growling and grovelling for a morsel of meat, or scrap of bread, and sharing it from the same bowl.

Nonetheless, I do have to grovel for *my* meal today. Yesterday, Peter told Ray and me, that he saw a man on a reindeer-drawn sleigh come into camp. No, it wasn't Santa (although we weren't far from his home) delayed in his parcel deliveries. He must have been a reindeer herder who came to barter with

Alex the cook for some canned goods because now, we are eating reindeer meat mixed in with our macaroni; all except me.

To my disappointment, my plate has nothing but macaroni, no meat. I think, with all the meals I was skipping when I was devouring Peter's supplies, the cook thought I didn't eat meat. I go back to the kitchen to grovel and try to make him understand that yes, I would like some meat. He obliges and gives me some, and, as expected, it's quite good.

Drilling is over and there is not much to do. I think we are all too tired mentally to get back to playing crazy rummy, as we did early on in our trip. As Peter, Ray, and I, head back to the shack, Bob lingers around the dining room, talking with Arthur and essentially hanging out there. He'll have to stay another night with the boys in the weather station room.

I think briefly about going out and adjusting the Canadian flag so that it's positioned upright, but I can't be bothered. What is done is done. Besides, someone may see me, and in a fit of patriotism, take it down.

As the afternoon approaches, it turns out to be a gorgeous day, with no wind, 0C, and thawing slightly. Mesha, Arthur's boss and the one with sore arms from the starter pulling contest he had with the DCP rig, decides it's time to put the shotgun to good use. He invites us over to the central area of camp to demonstrate his shooting skills and prove that the old shotgun isn't just a relic from WW1, but actually *does* works. And it *did*. It turned out to be fun to watch, not only because no one got hit or hurt, but also because he didn't miss a single shot, as he peppered holes into the remnants of the old outhouse. I don't know about a barn, but hitting the broadside of an outhouse was no problem for him. As he fired away, I just hoped he had checked to make sure no one was using the nearby, operational outhouse at the same time.

It reminds me of the story I once heard concerning Billy Martin, the fiery multi-time hired/ fired/hired manager of the New York Yankees baseball team, who used to go hunting with the legendary baseball star Mickey Mantle. Although they really did go hunting together, I don't know if the story I am relating to you is actually true or if it became folklore. I kind of think they made it up.

They went hunting one day. Mickey, knowing a farmer who would prob-ably let them shoot on his farm, tells Billy that he knows a place where they can go hunting. Upon arriving at the farm, Mickey tells Billy to stay in the truck while he gets permission from the farmer to hunt on his land. He heads to the house, talks to the farmer and gets permission, but the farmer has one request for Mickey. His donkey is old and lame and on its last legs, and could he possibly put it out of its misery and shoot it for him.

Mickey obliges, and says, "Sure."

On the way back, Mickey decides to play a trick on Billy. Pretending to be irate and mad, he comes storming back, huffing and puffing and tells Billy that his farmer friend, for whatever reason, isn't allowing them on the farm to go hunting.

"I'm so mad," says Mickey, "I'm going to go back there and shoot his donkey."

So he goes back behind the barn, shoots the donkey and puts it out of its misery, thus completing the farmer's request, and proceeds to bury it. A few minutes later he hears the blast from a gun nearby. He runs over quickly and there is Billy, with a rifle in his hand.

"What happened?" asks Mickey.

Billy replies, "Well, I was pretty ticked off as well with the farmer...so I shot his cow."

— * —

Talking about shooting, my dad, Dick, was a very good shot with the rifle. He had to be or my family and I would have been fatherless when I was about six years old. Dad loved hunting (whenever mom let him), and used to go hunting for deer or elk with my Uncle Pete and Uncle George.

In the mid-sixties, they went on a hunting expedition to Elk Valley, B.C. During the hunt, while separated, my dad was in some tall grass, stalking an elk. But little did he know a cougar was also stalking him. Apparently, the cougar was after the same elk, but saw dad as competition for the same prize. When dad heard something behind him, he turned around just in time to see the cougar leaping in the air to attack him. Dad got off a shot and hit it just before the cougar got to him. With the .30-06 jamming, as apparently they frequently do, he turned the rifle around, and, using the butt end, clobbered the cougar to make sure it was dead. It weighed over 160 pounds. It was considered one of the biggest cougars ever killed in B.C. at that time. Dad got the head mounted by a taxidermist.

Dad received a framed picture of himself holding the cougar head and the certificate he received with it. The certificate read:

Boone and Crockett Club

North American Big Game Competition

1965

This is to Certify that the

Cougar

entered by Dick Ritco

was awarded

Honorable Mention

Witnessed by [signature of witness]

For many years, in our recreation room downstairs, that framed picture adorned one of the walls. Next to this framed picture and certificate, was the mounted head of the cougar Dick shot. I think Dad always took pride of that trophy of his, especially considering that his life was in danger at the moment he shot the cougar.

In 2016, dad passed away. Since Uncle George's son, Ron, is an avid hunter, my sisters and I, decided to hand the cougar head, framed picture, and certificate over to him to be placed in his home in Grand Forks.

For us children, because we were so young at the time, I don't think we ever fully realized, or appreciated, the significance of our dad's achievement and of that one shot he took, of which, without, we could have been fatherless at that early age.

All I remember, is the many happy, summer nights of playing ping pong with my sisters, in that same rec room with the cougar, with its mouth displayed wide open, posing with a great growl, watching over us...with a spare ping pong ball in its mouth. It fitted inside its jaws just perfectly!

CHAPTER 21
LABYTNANGI

Thursday May 19
Day 23

This morning I didn't waste any time getting sentimental like I did yesterday. I sat silently on my bed, impatiently waiting to get the heck out of here and get going. We are physically and emotionally drained from the past two weeks of camp life and in need of some new adventures to perk us up.

Sure enough, the sounds of the helicopter came, and once again we went through the routine of dragging our luggage out to the landing area in preparation for a landing. We were more humble in our anticipation of a departure today. Even Gypsy's send-off duties were subdued and underplayed as if she thought, "This again? I did my farewell duties yesterday!" Nonetheless, she followed us reluctantly, lagging far behind us.

But we were rewarded, and the helicopter landed. This was it, our final goodbye. Assisted by the few Russians now left in camp, as most of them had left the last day or so to head to new "hunting for food grounds," we hauled our luggage on board. A few of the Russian drillers came along with us. Mr. Famienko and another Russian executive were on board to greet us as well. After quick, non-sentimental goodbyes to everyone, the helicopter lifted off, and we were on our way to new, uncharted adventures.

We gained altitude quickly, and within seconds the camp that held us captive for two weeks, was gone, nothing more than a few distant black specks contrasted against an ocean of white. We headed west over Baydaratskaya Bay, which was now breaking up considerably, with many areas of open water.

Looking out the tiny portholes, I saw the world below us, along with the memories it held, fade away, far off into the distance. For two weeks, our two cultures, the Russian and western worlds, had blended together having met, learned, lived and worked with, and come out somewhat more contented and richer for it. I was richer for this.

As I looked around, I compared the room I was in, to that of a confined flying compartment, not much bigger than our bedroom, flying through the sky. The image of enthusiastic, clean-shaven men seen a few weeks ago on the incoming flight was now changed to one of bearded, tired men all tuckered out. They sat on benches against the wall, seatbelts unfound, luggage, cargo, equipment all strewn about in a haphazard way, on the floor, amongst their feet. There was no warm beer or dried fish to partake of, this time around.

A short twenty minutes later, a shift in the pitch of the helicopter's engines indicated to us that we were over the bay and descending to the Flox weather station. We landed safely, and with engines still running, quickly got out to help unload some luggage, and then load John and Peter 2's luggage and assist them on board. Some of the Russian drillers that were with us were dropped off here.

As the engine rotors increased in power to lift off, we suddenly realized that, with all the noise and confusion of moving things on and off the helicopter, Ray wasn't on board. He was lost amongst those on the ground. With big Bob to the rescue, he quickly jumped out, grabbed Ray by the scruff of the hood, and hauled him back to the helicopter. With everyone now safely on board, we headed off to Labytnangi.

Over the next two hours, we sat quietly amongst the cargo, in sync with the gentle sway of the helicopter, as it surged forward. I was tired, and my mind overwhelmed to think about much, other than what might lie ahead for us. With my nerves strained, I was too wired to sleep. Besides, it was too noisy, even with the earplugs on. Everybody was off in his own little world of thoughts.

For Ray, John, and the two Peters from Holland, their jobs are finished. Once we have landed in Labytnangi, they will stay only a day or so, possibly look at the lab with us, and then fly to Moscow. From there, they will split off in different directions, the two Peters to Schiphol Airport in Amsterdam, and

Ray and John to Pearson Airport in Toronto and then on to Calgary. Bob still has to write the report on the drilling program and will fly to Amsterdam, then get ground transportation to the Heerema office in Leiden. He will meet up with Jim Oswell, the engineer from Calgary, who flew over a few days ago and is staying a few months in Leiden with his family. I will stay in Labytnangi for a week or so, observing, taking pictures, and note taking for my report of the laboratory. My visa expires at the end of the month. Quoting Blondie, "One way or another," arrangements will have to be made by someone high up, to extend my visa so I can stay the summer.

After landing in Labytnangi, the Russian drillers and our six man observation team were separated. Some of the Russians will move to their next jobs, while the others will head home to their families. We were driven to the same hotel that we stayed at on our way here. It was nice to be back to civilization.

I had my first shower since Moscow (about two and a half weeks ago). There is also a flush toilet. I am happy. We are back to civilization. The hotel here is about 47,000 rubles and 60,000 rubles with baths per person (double occupancy), about US$25 and US$35 respectively, and is very nice (it's the same one as before). It will be nice to not have to sleep on a dirty, squeaky cot.

Friday May 20
Day 24

Last night I had my first good sleep in weeks. Although it wasn't a *Sealy Posturepedic*, it sure beat sleeping on an old, rickety cot. Life just can't get any better than this. Today we devoted our time to the logistics of our demobilization. We are also in need of more money since we have spent a lot on hotel accommodations and meals, especially early on from our pre-camp era.

This morning, Mr. Famienko arrived with a local schoolteacher named Michael, who will also act as our interpreter. Michael, with the typical scholarly appearance, having dark rimmed glasses, beard, and moustache, introduced himself to us, and then all of us headed to the bank to exchange some US dollars for rubles. At the bank, each bill was scrutinized closely for counterfeits, and anything older than 1990 was rejected. Beginning that year, all US bills, other than the one and two dollar bills, had a security strip embedded in them that read, "U.S.A.," followed by the numerical denomination written in words. All our bills met with satisfaction and were accepted.

Concerning our departure arrangements, it was decided that the two Peters and John will fly out tonight by helicopter with Mr. Famienko to the Salekhard Airport, just a ten minute crossing over the Ob River. There, they will stay overnight at the airport hotel. The next morning, airline tickets for Moscow will be purchased for the Peters for them to fly out that day. Airline tickets for John, Bob, and Ray would be obtained for their transportation in a few days hence. John and Mr. Famienko would then return here to Labytnangi.

I am running out of money and will need some when I eventually leave for Moscow, whether it's in a week, or at the end of summer. I am getting weary of being here and certainly don't look forward to an extension of my visa for a summer "work" vacation here. Bob is trying to make arrangements to get money wired from Holland, but being so far north, with the remoteness of these communities, and its poor telecommunications, that's difficult to do.

With the business aspect of things now done, we headed back to the hotel room and had some snacks from what was left of our almost depleted supplies of granola bars and Nutribars. Later, our delightful hotel owner/host provided us with a nice assortment of pierogi, cucumber and tomato slices, and pickled fish for supper.

This evening we said our final goodbyes to Peter 1 and Peter 2, and a temporary farewell to John, who would be gone only for the night. Since it was a while since we last played, out came the cards, and the crazy rummy games started once again. There was no warm beer, nor heavy loaves of bread, placed on the empty chairs to replace those departed this evening.

Saturday May 21
Day 25

Today, Bob, Ray, Michael the teacher/interpreter, and I (John was not back yet from the Salekhard Airport) took a bus and went to Obskaya, a small town about twenty minutes away to see the laboratory facilities I had previously visited. But before we headed out, Bob took me aside to talk to me alone. He was aware that I strictly kept the Sabbath (Saturday), so he asked me if visiting the lab presented any problems to me concerning my faith. I considered the situation carefully, and thought it shouldn't be a problem, so I told him it was fine. It's a little dicey, and I suppose you could then argue, what *is* considered work? Strict religious sects who keep the Sabbath may disagree with me on this, but I made my decision, and I will leave it at that. I shall always appreciate the respect that Bob and Alex Costin gave me, concerning this subject.

In the early-seventies, as a teenager, I found out about Sabbath keeping, in a roundabout way, through Ron Lancaster, the legendary quarterback of the Saskatchewan Roughriders of the Canadian Football League. Throughout his career, Ron was known for his great ability to lead his team to victories, especially in the latter part of the game.

Back then, there was very little television coverage of football, and I had to share, with my sisters, the only radio we had. I was a great B.C. Lions fan, and still am today, and would sit on the couch downstairs in the dark basement, alone, and listen to the weekly game. Of course, the Lions, like my Vancouver Canucks hockey team, sucked, but I still listened enthusiastically. Immediately after the game, this nightly religious program would follow and I would "zap" the radio off; not interested. But one night B.C. was playing Saskatchewan and B.C., to my utter surprise and shock, was actually winning. It looked like they had the game in control. But of course, Ron Lancaster came to Saskatchewan's rescue and in the last minute pulled off a heroic "come from behind" victory, and my B.C. Lions continued their losing ways. I was so devastated and shocked that I didn't even bother turning off the radio. As I tried to comfort myself, and analyze the game as to what went wrong, the religious program was now airing. My attention turned to it, as the announcer was quite a bold speaker, and the subject matter was quite interesting. He was talking about Evolution and was offering free the booklet "Evolution: A Theory for the Birds." I listened for a while with interest, and then decided to order the magazine. After receiving the booklet in the mail a week later, and ordering a few more booklets over the next few months, I decided to join the church, and eventually became baptized.

Of course, over the years, as perhaps a lot of churches do, there was a disagreement in philosophy and beliefs, and a parting of ways for many. Despite this, I have managed to keep the Christian faith. I may be considered a lame duck to some with my beliefs, but I can't be bothered to let my feathers get ruffled.

So, to the "late", great Ron Lancaster, hats off to you, in unknowingly, leading me down this particular path in my Christian journey in life. But, at the same time, I still grit my teeth and grumble every time I think about that particular football game and every game that you played against my B.C. Lions...and won (which usually happened)!

Getting back to this trip, I always felt from Day 1 and onwards and still do today, that God wanted and allowed me to go to Russia. Doors were opened, and I was presented with opportunities throughout my journey and its planning stages. People, like Alex Costin, worked hard behind the scenes to make sure they could accommodate me. Alex bent over backwards for me, not only concerning my religious beliefs, but also ensuring I would get paid like everyone else. Even though I never did fly out each weekend, and things constantly changed in Russia as per usual, it was the thought that counted and the efforts that he took for me that I shall always remember and appreciate.

Having been to the lab previously during the first part of the journey, I remembered a benchmark that would help me know which bus stop to get off at. It was a bus stop with a broken brick wall behind it. After the bus made its rounds, making its customary stops, I saw the bricks knocked out of the walls on one, so I told everyone this was it. But unbeknownst to me at the time, there happened to be more than one bus stop, along the route, that had a broken brick wall behind it. We got off. Within less than five seconds, I was lost. I had no clue where we were. I had no more reference points to go by since all the buildings looked the same. After wandering around the wet, knee high, grassy tundra for about half an hour, we finally found the laboratory, a long rectangular building just over a hundred feet long with old, wooden, green walls. Or so I thought it was the lab.

We knocked on the door and waited. No response. After a few more minutes of knocking, we tried opening it. To our surprise, it opened. It was unlocked. But more surprising was the fact that it was totally empty and devoid of human life. It was just one big, empty building, perhaps home to the odd rat or two.

My first thought (it really was!) was that we were duped. It was a big con game. The people who pretended to be lab personnel, had actually staged a fake lab, briefly in appearance only, and then took the money and ran with it. But when my brain recovered from the shock of our discovery, I realized that that was a bonehead conclusion. I had to admit we were in the wrong building and still lost.

When this community was created, little imagination was involved, and all the buildings were built the same way; all painted with a dull, green paint and with the same size, more or less. All the bus stop walls seemed to have been designed and built with the same life span before they all tumbled down at the same time. I was sure glad Humpty Dumpty didn't live here in this town; otherwise, he would sure have a sore ass. So I really couldn't be blamed for screwing up, as I tried to console myself and figure out how to get out of this mess I put everyone into.

Once again, we went out into the fields and trampled it down in search of the "lost" laboratory. It was a good thing that the tundra wasn't being used to feed the local reindeer; otherwise they would have starved to death. After wandering aimlessly for another twenty minutes we finally found, what I cautiously thought, might be the lab. It was. Whew!

We introduced ourselves, and I was reacquainted with Roman, Tatyana, and the rest of the personnel. They didn't ask us why we were late. Roman and Tatyana are the lab managers while Ura, Sasha, and Anton are the technicians. We toured the lab for about two hours, and I took some more pictures. After the tour, we thanked everybody and said our goodbyes. I, of course, would be working with them sometime over the next few days, observing their laboratory equipment and work methods.

We didn't have any difficulty finding our way back to the bus stop. Just like the native Indians of North America did in the past century, we retraced our footsteps through the flattened grasses back to the road. Even *I* couldn't have got lost again, with the wide path now in front of us. Perhaps if we had been a little more creative with our walking patterns in the first place, the flattened area we left behind would have been interpreted by the self-named experts as a *crop circle* from the air, and this town would have become famous.

At the bus stop we waited for the bus to take us back to the hotel. While waiting, I gazed back at the wall, the one with a few bricks missing, and the one that had given me so much trouble. It smiled at me. I gave one of the loose bricks, lying on the ground, a few kicks and cussed it gently, just to let it know I wasn't too impressed.

The old, rickety bus came, and we paid our fare of 500 rubles (25 cents) and headed back to the hotel, with me hoping never again to see that nameless bus stop and its broken brick walls.

CHAPTER 22
MISSED OPPORTUNITIES

Saturday (cont.)
Day 25

After lunch back at the hotel, with John now back from the airport, Michael gave the three of us a walking tour of the town. Bob stayed back, to go over the drilling logs and perhaps get some rest.

Footnote: Michael bought us some post cards and books as gifts. We gave him some English books, as he likes to hone up on his English skills. I gave him Comstock Lode, a western novel by Louis L'Amour and a book on card games.

We walked around a bazaar where there were a few dinky food stores and shops selling local trinkets of sorts. Some of the food stores had sparsely occupied shelves of canned food, including canned fish, with a quarter inch of dust on them. We didn't buy anything. Other than that, there wasn't much in terms of fresh fruit or vegetables. The trinkets people sold in the streets were not the kind of cheap, metal crap that comes from other countries and pawned off as souvenirs of *named country*. This wasn't exactly a popular tourist resort for foreigners to visit in the first place. The trinkets consisted of essentially everyday items.

I saw a little old woman sitting against a wall, alongside the sidewalk, selling one tablespoon and two or three houseplants. Not a tourist souvenir spoon, but a simple eating spoon. That was probably all she had, trying to make enough money to buy herself another meal and stay alive for another day. It reminded me of the bible story of the poor widow who gave her two mites, which was all she had, to God and the temple. Except in this case, the old woman was hoping to *receive* a couple of mites just to stay alive. Her wrinkled face from a long life of toil portrayed a serene calmness, the one you have when you know that the death angel is just around the corner, and know there is nothing you can do, but accept it.

After wandering around for a bit, Michael brought us to a musical school where he taught. All the students were dressed to the hilt, in smart clothing and uniforms. The girls wore white blouses and black skirts while the boys had black dress pants on with white shirts and ties. It was wonderful to see them at their best, as we were introduced to them by Michael.

I felt out of place amongst these pretty, well-dressed young women and distinguished young men. But despite the grubby appearance we presented them, the girls, some of which were teenagers, all giggly and wide-eyed, and without hesitation, greeted us enthusiastically, speaking in their Russian language, happy to greet the foreigners.

Michael explained to us why everyone was dressed up. In twenty minutes time, they were giving a year-end musical performance for their parents and teachers. We were invited to stay and watch. Again, talking about timing! I would have loved to have stayed and watch them perform. It would have been a great cultural experience to see and hear them sing in their native language, with some playing the piano, or flute, or other musical instruments. It would have been fantastic!

Unfortunately, we had a meeting back at the hotel with Mr. Famienko concerning the drilling project. Despite the fact that this meeting didn't concern me, and I didn't have to attend, there was no way I could have stayed. With the long walk back, and typical of my style, I would surely have gotten lost again. With few people in town who spoke English and with Michael not available to baby sit me, I had to forgo this once in a lifetime opportunity.

When I look back on my life, there are two things that stand out that I regret the most of not doing or seeing. This was one of them. But the reality was, this was out of my control, so I just have to accept this.

The second major regret I have, which I *did* have control over, was not attending a performance in Calgary from one of my favourite singers, Blondie.

In the late 1980s, Deborah Harry's hard rock and roll style of music was softening, and she was moving into the genre of avant-garde jazz. During this time, one Saturday afternoon, she was performing at one of the local taverns in the heart of downtown Calgary. Being a shy person, I hesitated, not wanting to sit there by myself in the tavern, having a beer, alone. But if that was today, absolutely! No hesitations. It would have been fabulous to see her.

I did actually drive downtown, park my car, and walk down the street to the tavern and stop just outside the doors. Should I go in by myself and sit there alone? Would the joy of listening to my favourite singer outweigh the self-conscious doubts I had about myself. Sometimes our lack of confidence prevents us from simply enjoying life.

The tavern door beckoned me. The door was physically and symbolically there for me to open it. It was just ten feet away...and I walked away.

I missed out on what probably would have been a great afternoon of enjoyable jazz music from my favourite performing artist, Blondie.

I have always regretted that decision I made. Live life to the fullest! I didn't do it that day.

CHAPTER 23
THE LABORATORY

Sunday May 22
Day 26

Today we spent the day at the hotel simply relaxing. With only four of us left, with the two Peters gone, we were no longer interested in playing cards. We were tired and all wanted to go home, although I will have to stay at least another four days at the lab. The bosses still have to figure out what to do with me. Should they try to make visa extensions here, while I am still here in Labytnangi, or should I go back to Moscow? Ard and Ron, from Heerema, want me to stay all summer, but telecommunications here in Labytnangi and the far north are very poor. If my visa extensions fail, I will have to leave immediately for Moscow, and then go from there. The last thing you want to happen is to be stuck in a small Siberian town, in the middle of nowhere, with an expired visa. All travel by plane, train, bus, and hotel bookings can't be done without one. The authorities certainly wouldn't be happy if that situation ever arose.

Mr. Famienko talked it over with Bob and decided to arrange a ticket for me to leave at the end of the week. We could always delay it if we could extend my visa while I was here. At the same time, they would get airline tickets for Bob, Ray, and John. The latter two would leave immediately for Moscow, and eventually home to Canada. Bob would go to Amsterdam and then Leiden, where he would write his overall report at the Heerema office.

This evening, along with Mr. Famienko and Michael, we walked to a new restaurant for supper. Very modern and western style, it catered to Americans and those working overseas in the oil and gas industries. Mr. F. brought with him some Italian liqueur, vodka, and chocolates as he toasted the success of the project with us. Michael brought his large, bulky video camera, the one with the full-sized VHS tapes, and filmed us as we celebrated, laughed, and goofed the night away. The next day, Michael brought a copy for us and gave it to John. Although John promised he would make copies of it for everybody, I, nor anyone else for that matter, ever did receive one. I would have loved to see it. Then again, perhaps it's just as well. Who wants to see a video of themselves looking like a fool?

Four Russian men dressed in suits and ties, sitting next to us, saw our celebrations, raised their drinks of vodka to us, and toasted us as well. It was an evening of unwinding and celebration for us; and, of course, being stupid.

Monday May 23
Day 27

Today, the six of us, including Mr. Famienko and Michael, drove to the airport (helipad) in Labytnangi to see Bob, Ray, and John off. At the terminal, while we were waiting, Bob reached into his pocket and produced my airline ticket to Moscow dated for Friday, four days from now, that I will use at that time if necessary. He also added, looking me straight in the eye, "Just remember, I'm your boss, and you can call me anytime on the satellite phone if you have any issues." I immediately got the drift of what he was saying. He was there to defend me. Whatever decisions I decided to make, he was there to back me up.

As I pocketed the ticket, Ray added, "Make sure you don't get off at the wrong airport. There is one stopover before Moscow and don't get off there." I assured him I wouldn't make that mistake. I wasn't that dumb. "Trust me I know what I'm doing," I replied. Little was I to know that those were my last infamous words to him.

I said my goodbyes to everyone, as they abandoned me, on that lonely, overcast day. Now, I was alone, out of my comfort zone, to fend and make decisions for myself. Of course, I had my Russian friends who would still be here overseeing me, but generally, from now on, I'd make the decisions by myself. I had to accept that.

Earlier in the day, at a discussion at breakfast, Mr. F. offered that I could stay with him for the rest of the week, as I worked at the lab. I'm sure the meals and living quarters (not to mention the toilet facilities), would have been much better staying with him, but that presented the problem of having to take a bus each morning and evening to the lab. As I mulled it over, I suddenly remembered the misadventures I had a couple of days ago, with my penchant for getting lost using the wrong bench markers, since everything looked similar. On top of that, I didn't want to come face to face with that same bus stop that mocked me. I decided I would stay at the lab.

I think it was a fair decision. Despite the gloomy physical conditions that the laboratory presented, and its overflowing outhouse, Roman and Tatyana more than made up for it with their kindness and hospitality they showed me over the next few days I spent there with them.

— * —

Unless you have a white lab coat, wear black, square-rimmed glasses, and hold a clipboard in your hand when you work, I'm sure my descriptions of the laboratory tests would bore you to death, so I won't bother with the details. Instead, I will focus on the living quarters and its people.

The laboratory is in a long, rectangular building approximately one hundred and twenty feet long and thirty feet wide. Tenants occupy some rooms while the others lie dormant. There are about fifteen windows on each side, with a long hallway running down the center of it. It sits on the open tundra, along with many other buildings of similar style and size, hence my defensible argument as to why I mistook the first one we visited, for the lab.

A blue pipeline about three feet in diameter, perhaps transporting gas, sits elevated a few feet above the ground, propped up on wooden blocks, preventing it from sinking into the semi-frozen ground.

The place is dreary, amenities primitive, and the people, generally poor. Electricity is available only to those who can afford it. Food is very basic, and scarce, for those who don't have the means to support themselves. The man next door ate Tatyana's dog. There are no cats in the area, as the dogs have eaten them.

The outhouse is putrid with just a hole cut in the wooden, slatted floor. A horrific stench emanates from the two-foot high pile of poop that's overflowing. Scattered feces lie everywhere. I gagged the moment I entered this lone structure. It sits in the open for the community's use, and with twenty-four hours of daylight, pooping outside, without being seen, is not really an option. My peeing will just have to be done outside next to it. I am not looking forward to spending a possible summer (work) vacation here. As it turned out, I only stayed for four days, and I never used the outhouse once. There are no shower facilities, but I found out later from Roman, there was a community shower facility from which we could partake in for a small fee. I never used that either.

— * —

A driver took me to the laboratory where they dropped me off. Bob and Ray graciously decided to unload most of their heavy suitcases of technical books upon me, adding to my already overloaded suitcases I had. Perhaps they didn't want to be bothered hauling them back, or perhaps they thought I needed them (which I didn't), for my report. If I was brave enough, I'd have made up a story, and got rid of them by tossing them into the Ob River. It would have served them right for burdening me. I ended up with the hassle of carrying them through airports and eventually having a nightmare with them in Moscow.

Roman showed me to my bedroom, a nice room with two beds, and a table in the middle, next to a window. It wasn't too bad. I never ventured to the personal rooms of the others, but I assume they were adequate accommodations, and similar to mine.

After I settled in, Roman called me over to have lunch. The dining and kitchen areas were simple, with four wooden chairs next to the table and a small twelve-inch black and white television set sitting on the edge of it.

Tatyana boiled us each an egg and made the three of us some thin soup with large chunks of fish in it, simple, but not too bad. We were also served tea. I suppose the other technicians took care of themselves and ate elsewhere, because I rarely saw them, other than when they were working. Everyone working here is from the Petersbourg Expedition. With the language barrier between us, our meal was eaten in relative silence, but a comfortable one; not the awkward kind where you are trying to find something to say to break the ice. I was comfortable with them. Both Roman and Tatyana are middle-aged and have easy going personalities. I take it that they are not married and simply have a working relationship at the lab.

While we ate, we watched women tennis, perhaps Wimbledon although I wasn't sure, on the tiny television beside us. I'm not really a tennis fan. All I remember is that every lunch hour at the table, we usually watched a French woman playing and winning. (It actually was the French open, and was Mary Pierce, whom we saw most of the time. She ended up being the runner up to Arantxa Sanchez Vicario of Spain.)

For dessert, Tatyana treated us to two cookies, the packaged kind. Although they weren't homemade, they were still a treat, nonetheless. I missed having cookies and pastries at the weather station (even though I think those delights were smuggled in and eaten behind our backs...not that I'm holding any grudges against the suspects).

After lunch, I spent the rest of the day between watching the technicians doing work and going back to my room to write notes for the report and taking naps. The tests they worked on included consolidation, creep, thaw settlement, and frozen triaxial. Everyone was helpful and friendly. Every time something new was taking place, the technicians would come to my room and tell me to follow them and watch. They didn't have to take time to explain the tests to me because I was quite familiar with them. They just wanted to show their methodology of doing things, which I was to include in my report.

I found Roman to be quite intelligent and enthusiastic about his work, and he loved explaining his theories to me, even though I was hopelessly lost trying to understand them. Even without the language barrier between us, I wouldn't have understood.

In general, I found the Russians, throughout my trip, to be quite open with their thoughts, regardless of whether it had to do with politics, philosophy, religion, or any subjects that might have been taboo in the past. They expressed themselves freely, not afraid to speak out. Later that afternoon, Roman needed to phone his boss back in Moscow. Since they didn't have one, he asked me if he could use the satellite phone. I obliged.

After opening the briefcase, I pulled it out, hoping I could remember the instructions Bob gave me as to how to use it. We needed two things before we could use it, an electrical outlet and a south-facing wall. We had the electrical outlet, but our lab and living quarters were at the north end. Nonetheless, we set it up and tried, but couldn't pick up any satellite signals. We walked to the end of the hall, and Roman knocked on the door of the tenant to get permission to use his outlet. With permission granted, we tried once again. We got two satellite "pings", but couldn't make the connection. We gave up, walked back to our side, and had a quiet, uneventful evening.

CHAPTER 24
ROMANCE

Tuesday May 24
Day 28

Today I quietly spent observing and taking notes, as Ura, Sasha, and Anton did consolidation and triaxial tests. They also took readings on thaw settlement tests as well.

Yesterday Michael arranged for me to meet a colleague friend of his. His lady friend is a divorcee with a seven-year old daughter. He assured me she is very beautiful. At six o'clock this evening, he was to bring her over.

I was intrigued! I wasn't quite sure what his intentions were. Sometimes with the cultural differences that we have, the intentions can be somewhat convoluted and not understood outright. Was this intended to be a casual evening of a friendly nature, or was he trying to be a matchmaker and initiate a romance? I had visions of us walking down the garden path amongst the beautiful trees and flowers, with Michael, the chaperone, following exactly ten paces behind, making sure that no hanky-panky, such as the forbidden hand-holding, was going on. In our case, it would have been more of a cold stroll on a bleak Siberian landscape, devoid of any vegetation, except for the tundra, which would be flattened once more, eliminating the plans of any future reindeer herder for this area, and bringing about the arrival of more crop circle theorists from around the world.

Perhaps this *meeting* would lead further down the path to romance. Would she be pretty? What was the definition of "pretty?" according to Michael.

This evening, at the appointed time, I sat and waited outside on the door-steps of our "army barrack like" building.

I think a lot of times we are too serious to simply enjoy the mysteries and uncertainties that life offers us, especially when it comes to romance. It should be fun. But just the same, I was a bit out of my comfort zone. Often, it's the thoughts of making a fool of ourselves that makes things difficult emotionally. But this was an opportunity for me to have a fun date, and I should try and enjoy it to the fullest. Besides, it's kind of neat when I can tell everyone back home that, the first day after everyone had left for home, I had a Russian date. I was moving fast. I notice a lot of times in life, romantic encounters, like this one, occur when you least expect it.

A few years ago, I had a light-hearted flirt when I took some basic computer programming courses to hone my skills for work. Over the course of a couple of winters, I took four courses, each three weeks long. In the first couple of courses that first winter, there was a very pretty lady who also attended. With long blonde hair and brown eyes, she always sat at the opposite corner of the room. Although quite attractive, I was the least bit interested because I wanted to focus on getting good grades in the course (which I eventually did get). I enjoyed the courses and have always enjoyed doing computer related things.

I never did meet her that first year during the two courses I took. However, in the next year, in the fourth and final course I took, at the first night of class, I was the last one to arrive and there was only one seat left, next to her. We chit chatted the usual. Her name was Joanna M. and she actually grew up in the Okanagan Valley, as I did, but in Kelowna. We continued our casual conversation for a bit, and then the session started. After an hour or so, we had a twenty-minute break to get our required books at the bookstore half a block away. Not wanting to make her feel compelled to walk with me I delayed in tucking away my notes in my briefcase. But to my surprise, when I did head out, she was there, at the back of the room, waiting for me to escort her to the bookstore.

Over the next few weeks, we had good conversations, and got to know each other better, as we continually sat next to each other. That's another interesting quirk with human nature. We are creatures of habit. For some reason, it seemed that in every class I took, everyone sat in the same desk, as if their names were planted there. Not sure why we do that. Perhaps we are ingrained with that concept early on from our elementary school days.

But the funny thing was, on a couple of occasions, I had to miss class for work or other reasons, and by coincidence, unknown to me at the time, she missed class those same two times. She told me afterwards about those coincidental timings, and said that the others in the classroom noticed our M.I.A, and rumors were flying that we were a couple.

We both had a good laugh. It certainly would have been nice to have a romance with her, but I didn't enquire about her "availability status." Being quite attractive and all, I'm sure she had a boyfriend. Thus, our little flirtation ended. No romance, just a nice friendship, made unexpectedly by taking a computer night course. You never know who you'll meet when taking an education course or engaging in some church function or social activity. It might just be your future mate.

A more serious romantic encounter came during a time in my life when, once again, I wasn't the least bit interested. I was going through a mid-life crisis, and was focused on personal issues.

In the late '80s, A.R. was a summer student working under my supervision, at the soils laboratory in Calgary. Small in stature, she had short blonde-reddish hair, blue eyes, and freckles. I spent the summer teaching her, as she assisted me with the lab tests. She had average looks, or so I thought at the time. But as the summer went on, I found a strange attraction to her. I didn't want to call it "love" because I didn't want to get involved emotionally. I was still trying to figure out what I wanted to do with my life.

But as the days went by, that emotional barrier wore down and by summer's end, I was smitten. I found that any time she didn't show up for work because of sickness, I was hopelessly lost and empty. Her beauty had grown and she exuded magnetism. Simply being in the same room with her was powerful, as I could feel her presence. We could sense, non-verbally, by body language, each other's thoughts, or when one of us was down and having a bad day. I ended up having a few wonderful dates with her, but, unfortunately, because of my awkwardness and shyness, wasn't able to communicate my deepest affections to her.

Looking back, I'm sure she was exasperated with me in not conveying my true feelings to her. We ended with a quiet, unspoken parting of ways. It was a lack of communication on my part. I still regret that to this day. She is a wonderful lady.

— * —

In the end, I was stood up. Michael and his lady friend never showed up. After waiting for an hour, I headed back inside to my bedroom. Oh well, that's life, these things happen. Michael never had the opportunity to tell me directly what happened, but I kind of knew and figured it out right away.

Transportation and communication, whether by vehicle, bus, or telephone is very poor or non-existent here. Michael needed to borrow a vehicle, since he didn't have one, and so probably couldn't obtain one. And with few people having phones, he had no way of communicating this to me.

I found out about the problems everyone goes through here early today, when Roman had to go into town to make his phone call to Moscow. What would have taken us just a few minutes back home, took him most of the day. He had to walk a fair distance to the bus stop, perhaps endure a long wait there, with its limited service out here, take it into town many kilometers away, find a place that had a telephone and then take the same bus, with its multitude of stops, back home. After leaving this morning, he didn't arrive back until late afternoon.

I wasn't upset with Michael or anything like that. This was just the everyday harsh realities of the life they lived and had to put up with.

But still, at the same time, I wonder with slight amusement, what would have happened if Michael *had* arranged transportation, and arrived with his lady friend and her daughter? Amazing how one's life can change if only for a simple thing as to whether a vehicle or transportation is available at the time. Maybe my life would have changed dramatically. Maybe my single airline ticket for home would have been increased to three, Ray and Bob's luggage dumped into the Ob River, and I would be bringing home my new set of luggage: "Hello everybody, meet Anastasia and Cassandra."

CHAPTER 25
FAREWELL MY FRIENDS

Wednesday May 25
Day 29

I am quite tired. I guess maybe I worked hard getting pictures and observing. Many of the tests finished up today. I also beat the computer two of three. I played a few games of chess with Anton. They were all very good games. It was one win and one loss, although Roman helped me a lot in winning. I must sleep now. There is total daylight at this time of night.

(I realized)...What a difficult life people here, live in. These are basically army barracks with no running water and no toilet facilities. There is an out-house with a hole in the ground. Life with democracy is getting worse. There is 12% inflation/month. The man next door ate Tatyana's dog. No cats here. They are all eaten by dogs.

Thursday May 26
Day 30

Today, Thursday, is my last day here at the laboratory with my wonderful hosts. I will cherish forever the fine times I had with them. It was nice to share their meager lifestyle, and break bread with them. I enjoyed their fellowship and simple meals usually consisting of oatmeal porridge and tea for breakfast, and fish soup, a boiled egg, two cookies, and tea for lunch and supper. It was like a home away from home. I think these days I spent with them perhaps has given me the best reflection of what Russia and her people are really like. I experienced its hospitality, generosity, and soul. I found so often of those I met in Russia, that the poorer they are, the more they have to give, especially from the heart.

The days spent here are in stark contrast to that night when I first met Roman at the hotel, then walking silently alongside him, down that desolate road leading to nowhere. Now, instead of wanting to be "anywhere but here," I found it hard to leave, knowing that I was going home to a land of luxury, while they had to remain behind.

This evening, hidden under my bed blankets, I left them some canned food, small tools, souvenirs, playing cards, gifts, and about US$10.

Tatyana gave me her home address in Moscow. I showed them pictures of my relatives and family. It's kind of sad to think such wonderful people have to live in such poor conditions.

As so often is the case, when I got back home to Calgary, Canada, I once again became absorbed with the daily rituals of our fast paced, modern society and with the lavish entertainment it offers us. Although Tatyana gave me her home address in Moscow...I never did write her.

Friday May 27. 9:30pm.
Day 31

I am at the Salekhard Airport at the hotel (8,100 rubles each person, double occupancy, about US$4.50 per night). Nick paid. We are sharing. I gave all my gifts (souvenirs, tools, playing cards, and food) [and some money] *away to Roman and company. I said goodbye. They were all wonderful hosts. Mr. Famienko and Nick and a bus driver came and picked me up at 2:00pm. We went to the heliport (28,000 rubles/ticket. They paid). At 5:30pm, the helicopter took off. Again, they don't shut down. People just walk out to the helicopter and cram aboard, about twenty-five people, men, children, and women. They barely get on, shut the door, and they are off. No seat belts. The people stand right next to the exit. Flight is only across the river* [east] *to the town* [airport or heliport] *of Salekhard, about ten minutes away. Inside, the noise is deafening as usual. No one wears earplugs* *(or has them). Landed, and staying here at the hotel overnight. I tried to phone Holland, but couldn't receive a satellite (kept losing it).*

I hope someone will be there in Moscow to pick me up. Otherwise, I will play it by ear. I left instructions that if I couldn't reach them, to assume that my flight schedule was the same (they know time, etc.) of flight. It will be a busy and hectic weekend. We had boiled eggs, tea, and bread, all supplied by Nick. It was a nice clear day of about +1C.

Nick's job was to make sure I made it from the laboratory to the Salekhard Airport and onto the correct flight to Moscow. We are staying the night at the airport hotel and then he will see me off first thing in the morning. The first thing he did when we got to the hotel room was to prepare our supper. With the hotel room's teakettle, Roman filled it with water and set it on the gas stove to heat up and make some tea. He then fished into his pockets for two hard-boiled eggs, a small glass container of salt, and a teabag. Handing an egg to me, we both cracked ours open. Along with the simple tea without any cream or sugar for it, but with a little salt for our eggs, we shared our simple meal in silence.

Afterwards, to break the awkwardness of a silent and boring evening, Nick pulled out the universal language translator, the chessboard. As we played, to put it bluntly, Nick could easily see I was lousy. Many times he pointed out better moves for me to make, many of which, perhaps a hundred steps into the future, I would suddenly realize the brilliance of it. Needless to say, despite his help, Nick beat me three straight.

At this point of the trip, after thirty-one days, I was starting to make sense of what the Russians were saying, even if I didn't understand every word. Through the study of their gestures and inflections of their voice, I was apprehending their intentions and thoughts; but it did take a lot of mental energy. It wasn't until I got back home that I realized how stressed my brain was. And it certainly was a relief to get back to where the language was my own, and give my brain a rest.

CHAPTER 26
ALMOST LEFT BEHIND

Saturday May 28
Day 32

Today, I almost got left behind and could have become a Russian peasant for life. Images of borscht soup, cabbage fields plowed by oxen, and my new wife, world weight lifting champion Olga, nattering away at me for my incompetence, flashed through my mind, as I ran across the tarmac to catch the Aeroflot airplane.

After saying my farewell to Nick at the Salekhard Airport, I boarded the Aeroflot twin-engine plane. We took off and the flight started smoothly. After a couple of hours we landed at a small, non-descript town (I never did find out the name of it). When the plane came to a stop, the captain spoke something in Russian over the P.A. system as, at the same time, one of the flight attendants walked down the aisle, motioning everyone to get off. Everybody started to disembark. I hesitated. I was uncertain. Since this was a local, domestic flight, all communications were done in Russian. There was no English translation.

Remembering the words of Ray, "There is one stopover before Moscow and don't get off there," the last thing I wanted to happen was to get off and be stranded here, lost, alone. I waited until the last moment until everyone had departed and the flight attendant had to come over and "shoo" me off the plane.

As I walked on the tarmac amongst the local travellers, heading for the airport building, trepidation and chills went through me. I felt this same way when I was on that lonely walk with Roman when I first met him. I didn't want to be here.

I asked a few questions in English to those I walked with, hoping that someone understood. They conveyed that this was a temporary refueling stop. For safety reasons, everyone had to disembark while the plane was being refueled.

At this point, in brilliant hindsight, I should have paid more attention to whom I was walking with, and the people around me. I didn't realize that in about fifty minutes time or so, this was going to cost me dearly with a lot of panic, emotional turmoil, and a few more grey hairs. That is one of my problems. I don't pay enough attention to details when it matters the most. Typically, when I worked at Supervalu in Oliver a few years later, someone would ask me about something not on the shelves. After going back to the cooler to find out if we had it, I would often forget who I was talking to, and wander aimlessly about, asking the customers, "Was it *you* that I was just talking to about the cauliflower?"

"No."

"Sorry."

Inside the terminal, all signage was written using the Cyrillic alphabet, with no English equivalents, and no information centers. All announcements over the P.A. system were in Russian. Usually the waiting areas and ticket counters at any airport, regardless of country, are similar and found easily. But this airport confused me. I was lost.

As everybody wandered off in different directions, this, the final destination for some, while others hung around in the terminal, I decided to follow the tracks of one young lady whom I thought was on the plane with me, and might be heading to Moscow as well. I should be fairly safe following her.

Wrong, wrong, wrong! (She was simply shopping.) If there ever was a life changing experience and decision I made that almost forever changed my world, this was it!

I followed her around, making sure I didn't lose sight of her. She casually shopped, looking through the offerings of the bookstores and various shops. All during this time, I was listening hard to the paging system, trying hard to hear the words "Moscow" or anything related to my flight, but I couldn't make anything out.

After about forty minutes of woman stalking, I finally thought to myself, "Self, perhaps it's time to go to the main lounge area and make sure that my plane hasn't taken off without me." I walked over there and looked out the window. It was still there. That was a relief. Whew! But wait! Upon looking closer, I noticed the stairway ramp leading into the plane was gone, and the doors all closed. But not only that, the twin-engines at the back were revved up fully as the plane was about to taxi down the runway. Oh no, this did not look good! I was in trouble.

At this point in time, I would like to digress a bit. It's amazing how, when you are suddenly faced with an emergency, and panic sets in, how quickly your mind works at solving problems. Where, for forty minutes I was in a fog, aimless chasing Svetlana around the airport, now, I was suddenly able to adapt to the circumstances and find a ticket counter in about thirty seconds flat.

At the ticket counter, trying to catch my breath, I showed the lady my airline ticket and pronounced the word "Moskva," which is how they pronounce "Moscow."

I will never forget the look on her face as she looked at my ticket. Her face turned white in horror, and by her great multi-tasking abilities, was able to do three things at once. While screeching in a high-pitched voice, in her native language, at the lady next to her to get on the phone, she got on another phone as well, screaming out instructions to the person at the other end. At the same time, she had the ability to look scornfully at me, in all my innocence, and yell at me, pointing to the end of the hallway, which, with my masterful understanding of the Russian language by now, I assumed, confidently, to mean, "Run...quickly!"

And so I...*ran...quickly!*

I ran down the hallway, turned the corner to my left and ran up to the security screening area where the lone male security agent was yawning quietly, bored to death.

As usual, my metal belt buckles or Tic Tacs set off the alarm, so I stopped and waited for the agent to perform his customary search and "wand" me over. Although the Tic Tacs, because of their tin foil, caused me a lot of hassle going through airport security systems and setting off their metal detectors, they provided me with the only clean thing I had on me, fresh breath. Stinking clothes, dirty underwear, but at least I had fresh breath (commercial done, royalties please).

The security guy had this confused look on his face, the kind you have when you first wake up in the morning, so I didn't bother waiting for him (or waking him up). I kept running. Now, I was out the door of the building and running to a chain link fence, where a little old lady, about sixty-five years of age, was opening the gate for me.

Everywhere in Russia it seems, are little old ladies acting as security attendants; stores, malls, offices, airports, you name it. I guess they need to supplement their old age pensions. But at the same time I wonder, what happens if someone makes a break for it, or steals something. How were they supposed to catch them? Unless of course, they had a little scooter from which they could chase the culprit. But I never did see any scooters around.

As I ran through the gate, she yelled at me and gave me a good scolding, which I assume, meant something like "идиот." I'm sure if she had a stick or belt with her, she would have given me a whack or two across the ass, as I passed by her, onto the tarmac towards the plane.

In one of the episodes on *Seinfeld*, there is a scene where Kramer is running down the tarmac, trying to catch the plane, as it is taxiing. Well, that was me. Although the plane hadn't actually moved yet, its engines were revved fully, and the pilots were restless, as they wanted to get going.

As I continued my now exhausting run, I saw the luggage cart with my luggage "solo" on it being towed away from the plane. But now they were signalling it to return. The ramp at the back of the plane, between the two engines, had now been lowered for me to get on.

At this point, my adrenalin rush which started when I first heard the words, "Run, quickly" (English equivalent) from the ticket lady, was fading fast and my energy depleted. As the cart turned around, I lunged for it and just managed to grab hold of it and jump on. I didn't wait for it to stop, I just jumped on. Come to think of it, that might have been the first and only hitchhiking I have ever done in my life, albeit without the person's permission.

As we approached from the rear, the twin rear engines continued to spew out their fire. The pilots had no thoughts whatsoever, of shutting them down, even just briefly, as I boarded. I just hoped I wouldn't get burned in the process. After throwing my luggage into the back compartment, I entered from the rear as well. I took a moment to catch my breath and decompress. The last few minutes had been quite hectic. I quietly rearranged my rumpled clothing, tucked in my shirttails into my pants, and adjusted my belt. After taking a deep, calming breath, I casually walked down the aisle to my slightly amused, but quiet, fellow comrade passengers. They were too polite to laugh at me outright.

Sometimes in life, there are moments when you simply want to bury yourself under a blanket, or hope you were a million miles away, like when my chair broke in church. This was, again, one of those moments. On the outside, I tried to look calm; on the inside, I was just dying.

I must tell you about that chair-breaking incident. This was when I started keeping the Sabbath, and the church would rent a high school gym on Saturday afternoons. I was quite new at the time, quite shy, and did not know too many people. I was sitting there quietly one afternoon, amongst the congregation, listening to Mr. Earle give his usual fiery sermon. The chair I was sitting on was probably kind of old, and it creaked and sagged. Nevertheless, I was not too concerned. In fact, I confidently had both feet off the floor resting on the chair in front of me, thus having my full weight of my body on the chair. As I squirmed about, as my arse was getting sore, the chair creaked and sagged lower. I thought to myself, "Wouldn't it be embarrassing if this chair broke. With it being metallic and all, and with the hard gym floors and echoing walls magnifying the sounds, it would probably create a huge noise and sound wave." But I didn't think too long about it. I returned my focus to Mr. Earle and his sermon. He was on a roll.

About thirty seconds later, almost timing perfectly to the climax of his exhortations to his captivated audience, a huge explosion rocked the gymnasium. "Kaboom!" I was stunned! I didn't know what happened at first. Perhaps the shock waves may have concussed me slightly. But there I was, flat on my ass, the focus of three hundred startled people as they looked around to see what had interrupted their note taking. It took me a few seconds to realize that that explosion came from *me*, with my chair exploding underneath me.

Perhaps, in hindsight, I should have taken the chair's warnings, with its squeaks and squawks, to heart, and not been so arrogantly dismissive of what it was trying to tell me. Luckily, there was an empty chair beside me to sit on, so I didn't have to wander aimlessly about, searching amongst many upset people whom I had disturbed their peace. Even Mr. Earle at this point kind of mumbled something into his mic about maybe keeping the sermon short for the day.

I could have died of embarrassment. I wished I were a million miles away at that moment. I dusted my suit and pants and slunk into the empty chair nearby. We left the demolished chair in its place, ready for the dumpster afterwards. I hoped I wouldn't have to pay for it. Untypical of my strength tests I did at the laboratory on soil, I did a strength test on the new chair to make sure it was sound. It seemed to be capable of holding a load bearing of about two hundred pounds, which my body weighed. I gently sat in it...but with both feet firmly on the floor this time.

Back to my Russian flight. Later on, as I tried to stay low and blend in with everyone else, the stewardess came along, offering drinks, or juice from a tray. Not thinking, as I was still self-absorbed with my embarrassments of a few minutes ago, I grabbed the whole tray from her rather than just taking one of the glasses. Instantly realizing my faux pas, I quickly took a glass of juice and returned the tray to her, as she gave a look that said it all, "Aye yi yi," as her eyes rolled to the heavens. Where is my security blanket?

I was so embarrassed by this airport incident, in this unknown town, that I never told anybody about it until four years later, when I met Adele Sanoy, whom I became good friends with. Having lunch with her one day in the town of High River, Alberta, I finally had the nerve to tell someone about those misadventures I had. Surprisingly, she didn't laugh at me. In fact, she seemed rather nonchalant about the whole affair. She even went to the extent of suggesting that I write a book about my trip to Russia. Perhaps she could see I had enough adventures, and misadventures, to fill a book. So, with breakneck speed, much like that of the perpetual tortoise that Mrs. Hopkins, my first grade teacher, compared me to, I went ahead and followed her advice. Of course, it only took me almost twenty years to the day to get around to it!

— * —

But I have learned over the years that no matter what our life experiences are, good or bad, rewarding or humiliating, they are great to have. It's better to have them than simply live a safe, conservative lifestyle. It took me four years to have the courage to revisit and relate my experience to someone. But now, I can look back and laugh at those moments, even though, at the time, I could have died of embarrassment.

I thank God for giving me that moment in time and the resulting memories from it. But still, at the same time, I again have to wonder, with slight amusement, what my life might have become if I did get stranded there, at that unknown town.

Perhaps the Russian peasant lifestyle isn't so bad after all. I like Borscht soup. My cousins George and Robin Ritco make excellent Borscht, as I found out when I visited them in Grand Forks, B.C. in 2017. I have a Russian connection on my father's side, with relatives still living in Russia and the Ukraine. And I remember our dad speaking Russian to us kids, when we were bad and deserved a spanking. As far as the cabbage fields being plowed by oxen, I think they, for the most part, are plowed using the modern "Boris Steele" tractors, the Russian equivalent to ours.

And perhaps, best of all, Olga, instead of being world weight lifting champion, was the opposite; a "Natasha," a beautiful, slim, soft-spoken figure skater champion, the girl that most single men, like myself, dream of.

Maybe my airline ticket would have been torn up, Ray and Bob's luggage once again thrown in the Ob River, and I would have stayed. Like Omar Shariff's character in Dr. Zhivago, right now I would be snuggling next to Natasha, happily content, trying to stay warm on a frosty Siberian night; a menagerie of glittering icicles hanging down the edges of the roof of our frozen mansion, as it stood alone in the vast, frozen, mystical heartland of Russia's Siberia.

I can only dream...what if?

CHAPTER 27
DO NOT LEAVE MOSCOW!

Saturday May 28 (cont.)

The rest of the trip to Moscow was non-eventful in the sense that I didn't make a fool of myself anymore. At the Bykovo Airport, as previously planned, in the event I didn't phone, it was assumed I would be on the flight. Sasha was there to pick me up. The first thing he did was hand me a telex that read, in bold letters:

DO NOT LEAVE MOSCOW!!!

CALL ARD DOORDUYN OR JIM OSWELL AT HOME ASAP!!!

(They enclosed their phone numbers as well.)

I knew by the urgency of the letter, that Ard was a little ticked off at me. At this point I need to explain. Back at the laboratory in Obskaya, Bob had left me with the satellite phone to call Holland and update Ard on what was happening at my end. Ard was ticked off because I didn't contact him prior to leaving, even though I tried. Although my visa was expiring in a few days, at the end of the month, they wanted me to stay all summer long at the laboratory there (Obskaya), observing. They were confident they could take care of my visa at their end to extend it. Meanwhile, the backup plan if things didn't go as expected, and my visa couldn't be extended, was for me to fly back with the airline ticket Bob had given me to Moscow, and go from there.

I *did* try to phone Holland via the satellite phone, but, of course, you need electricity to power it up, and a south facing wall to try to connect to a satellite flying over at the time. Our lab was at the wrong end, so one day I knocked on the tenant's door at the end of the hall to ask him if I could use his electrical outlet. No one answered. After waiting a while, and after knocking some more, I gave up. (In retrospect, I was glad that no one answered because it offered me the excuse that at least I tried. Also, in retrospect, it was a good thing because, as I mention later in this chapter, it's virtually impossible to extend your visa while here in Russia.)

As far as we knew, no one else around the community had a telephone, so the satellite phone was the only option to make contact. At that point, I decided to carry out the backup plan and take the flight back to Moscow, as prearranged, and hope Sasha was there to pick me up, which of course he was.

Another thing that Ard didn't seem to understand was that Obskaya was in a remote, primitive area of Siberia (come to think of it, actually most towns are in primitive areas in Siberia), with few telephones or means of communication. Yet, somehow, he figured, perhaps with a magic wand, or dog sled, he could arrange for a visa to appear suddenly at the doorstep of the lab the next day and solve all our problems.

You don't want to be trapped in a foreign country, especially Russia, without a passport. The authorities do not take it lightly. You can't travel by train or plane, you can't stay in a hotel you can't do anything. You are stuck. Actually, when we did go to the foreign embassy in Moscow a few days later, we found out we could not extend it anyways. It appears that, regardless of whether a person is a visitor or on business, they cannot extend their visa while in the country. They have to exit, then re-enter with a new one. Therefore, it was good that I got out of Russia when I did, before my visa expired.

On top of this, staying the summer would have been fruitless, a total waste of time. All the observations of the laboratory, the work methods, the personnel, the equipment, were all completed in the first week of my stay. There was nothing else to do or accomplish. I would have died of boredom, and I don't know what I would have done with the toilet issues and the outhouse. I guess looking on the positive side of things, with the poop hole filled and overflowing, there was no chance of me losing my toque down the hole, as Peter did.

Like the title of the 2001 movie, *The Fast and the Furious* starring Paul Walker and Vin Diesel, *that*, described us, as Sasha drove us through the streets of Moscow. Sasha drove *fast*, while I was *furious*, as he took too many chances once again. I knew that I had to make an urgent phone call to Ard, but that could wait a little while longer, at least as long as I stayed alive.

But, for some mysterious reason, what turned out to be a blessing in disguise for me in the end, and perhaps by the grace of God, Sasha drove me to the wrong hotel. After checking at the front desk, they found no record of any reservation for me. After making a phone call back to the Heerema office, Sasha realized I was supposed to have been taken to the *Radisson* hotel. This was the *Radisson Slavyanskaya* hotel. Even though this one was much more extravagant, and probably more expensive, they decided to book me here anyways.

The Radisson Slavyanskaya is a very modern western style hotel with accommodations of the major U.S. media outlets; CNN, ABC, and others, who use it as one of their main headquarters in Moscow. English is widely spoken.

After months of renovations, the hotel had just completed, within the last hour of my arrival, complete upgrades to all their executive suites. I was the very first one to be registered in one of these suites, and for the rest of the evening, no one occupied that floor but me. Go figure. Talk about the timing and this "accidental" misplacement I had, all because Sasha drove me to the wrong hotel. What blessings! Has to be more than a coincidence!

And to think, within a forty-eight hour period, I went from living in Siberia primitively with no telephone and no flush toilet, to a newly refurbished five-star executive suite in a hotel. That's pretty neat. Not many people can say they've experienced this.

The first thing I did, at the Radisson Slavyanskaya hotel, was to take my stinking clothes off and have a long, hot bath. It felt nice to be back to civilization, with its modern amenities. I should have done what some army personnel do when they come in from the field, and simply showered with my clothes on, thus cleaning them at the same time. However, I wanted to unwind and simply soak for a while. Afterwards, I tended to my laundry duties and got around to washing my dirty socks and underwear. After I turned into a prune, I got out of the tub and shaved as well.

Now was the time to see what was on TV and what I had missed. For almost five weeks, I was separated, isolated, in another world, having no idea what I was missing, or if World War 3 had started. It seemed like I "lost" five weeks of my life, especially when it came to the world of sports.

Turning on the big twenty-six-inch color television set, with its twenty or so channels, was a big change, compared to the small twelve-inch black and white one with its lone channel back in Obskaya. As I flipped through the channels, I came across quite a few American channels, including the mainstream news and CNN. After seeing the tail end of the world news and realizing that the world was still operating as normal, the sports broadcast was now on. What I heard next totally stunned me and a horrible feeling of homesickness came over me.

When I had left to go to Russia back in April, my favourite hockey team, the Vancouver Canucks, were losing three games to one to Calgary in the first round. I could accept that. After years of misery, I have learned never to get my hopes up too high for them.

"Wait until next year," as they say.

But here, the announcer was talking about the Vancouver Canucks about to start the Stanley Cup finals against the New York Rangers in a few days. What? They were behind badly in the first round. I assumed it was all over. Somehow, though, they managed to win the next three games, I believe all in overtime, with Pavel Bure scoring in the seventh game, the series-winning goal. After that, they went on to win the next two series before advancing to the finals to face the Rangers. I later found out they beat Dallas and then Toronto in five games each, to advance. I would have loved to have been transported a few weeks back in time and followed the Canucks complete journey to what might end up being their first ever Stanley Cup.

As I reflected upon this, I wondered what else I had missed during my departure from the so called "real world," but the news was the same old... nothing new.

But, I did notice that Moscow had changed since I first arrived here a few weeks ago. Previously, it was late winter, but now it was springtime. Trees were showing their youthful leaves, and flowers were in full blossom, boldly displaying their colors. Even the inside of the airport had changed and seemed friendlier and brighter. It's refreshing to realize that Moscow isn't a rundown city, but rather a city where its people are proud of its beauty and have taken the time to nurture it. The city had just taken the winter off for a little hibernation. Now it was in full display of what it had to offer, including its beautiful scenic parks, gardens, and architecture. No wonder the Russians are a very loyal and patriotic people.

After watching the television for a bit, I decided to make my unavoidable, dreaded phone call to Ard in Holland to plead my case as to why I flew back to Moscow without phoning him. With passion from both sides, Ard and I had a long discussion, explaining our differing points of view. I explained the difficult situation I was in and the difficulties of getting a call through. I also told him that there wasn't any point in extending my visa and staying the rest of summer. I had all the information I needed for my report. After I clarified these things with him, I think he finally understood the situation. But regardless, he still wanted me to stay put for the time being until they figured out what to do next. Over the next few days, our phone conversations were more cordial and relaxed, and focused more on arrangements for me to head to Leiden, Holland to finish my report.

After I hung up the phone, I decided it was time to so something that was in the weeks of waiting, my dirty laundry. Even though I'm sure the hotel had laundry service, I didn't bother. I filled the bathtub with plenty of hot water, threw in a small amount of detergent that I had brought with me, and threw my stinky underwear, socks, and shirts in there to soak. I also decided it was time to give my carry-on bag, with its now gaping rip across the top, its final resting place, the garbage bin. It had served its duty well, but books and things were constantly falling out, and it was no longer useable.

I then ordered room service consisting of chicken, orange pop, and black forest cake. After finishing my laundry and hanging them out to dry, my room service order came, and I settled down for the evening. I plopped myself on the comfy chair and flipped through the channels. I decided on a movie on the pay channel with Robert Redford and Demi Moore entitled *Indecent Proposal*. It wasn't too bad. And then it was lights out for me. This had been a long and hectic day.

Sunday May 29
Day 33

This morning I worked on the rough draft of my report and then decided to do a bit of exploring of the hotel itself. The Radisson Slavyanskaya hotel is also a business center and home to most of the television networks with their international audience. It has a business center that offers all office services including fax, desktop publishing, computer graphic design, phone rentals, and color copying services. There are three restaurants and a shopping mall.

I didn't venture outside the hotel since, to put it bluntly, I was too chicken. Included in the hotel's welcome sheet were some safety instructions concerning walking on the streets or taking a taxi.

"Always be cautious when out of the hotel and try to travel with someone when out at night. Do not use short cuts or take narrow alleys, or poorly lit streets. Before crossing a bridge or going into underground passageways, be alert to who is around you. If someone suspicious is behind you, stop to let him by and make eye contact with him to make him aware that you are alerted."

"Taxi – Make it clear to the driver that he is not to take on any other passengers during the drive. If the driver stops to make a phone call during the trip, get out, and take another taxi."

The safety instructions goes on to talk about a few other general safety precautions and about Gypsies, who are quite prevalent here and aggressive in their general tactics they use.

After 1988, the people of Russia were given more freedoms. However, a vacuum was created, from which the Russian mafia rose up and took advantage. At the time we were in Russia, in 1994, these new mafias were only in their infancy stages and not too prevalent.

A few years later, Alex Costin our initial logistics coordinator, went back to Russia on another work project. He told us afterwards that a few "shady" people came up to him offering their services for his protection while he was there. Whether they actually were with the Russian mafia or simply people who wanted to extort money from him, or both essentially being the same, he couldn't really tell. But he didn't succumb to their offers. He refused and basically told them to, "Go to hell."

Brave man!

Monday May 30
Day 34

This afternoon a driver from Gazprom picked me up at the hotel and took me to the Heerema office to work on extending my visa, as well as working on getting a provisional airline ticket for me. One interesting thing I noticed about company vehicles here in Moscow, and perhaps the rest of Russia as well, is that most don't incorporate company logos on their vehicles. I don't know if it's because there is a lack of signage companies around, or for safety reasons they don't want to be targets, or if they just don't care to advertise their services. Actually, come to think of it, that was the way with most stores, restaurants, and hotels throughout my travels here in Russia; very little signage advertising their services.

I was told simply to go outside the hotel and wait for a blue van with one person, the driver, in it. The blue van came, and I hopped in. It was the right one, luckily for me, and I wasn't taken somewhere and mugged. We drove to the office where I met Lidea, a secretary, who spoke good English and would help me.

Lidea is the chief secretary for the big boss, who was out of town for the day. I found her to be quite charming and friendly. As I spent the afternoon with her, I realized that secretarial duties in Russia, or at least at this office, are a lot different from ours in the western world.

Instead of having a desk with its corners filled with "in" and "out" trays and stacks of reports to be typed or filed, Lidea's desk was neat and tidy. Other than a perfectly stacked pile of papers off to one corner, and a telephone in the middle, that was it. Not a speck of dust to be found. She didn't even have a cup of coffee on it.

Sitting in her chair, leaning forward, she had her hands clasped together on the desk, waiting. She was expecting a very important phone call from her boss, who might phone at any time. It might be in a few minutes time, or it might be in a few hours, it didn't matter, the phone was absolutely off limits.

After talking with her and consulting with some of the engineers, it was decided to leave the work on my visa extension until tomorrow and instead, focus on arranging an airline ticket for me. But since the airline ticket involved using the phone, it would have to wait until the boss called. I chatted with one of the engineers, Sergei, and asked him to look over a Russian Standard that was in Russian, that I received from Roman. I wanted to know if thaw settlement tests were included in it.

As I sat in front of Lidea, waiting, I was impressed by her patience. She was perfectly content to sit there and wait, no book to read, couldn't be bothered with coffee or tea; just sit there waiting patiently for the one phone call that would complete her work duties for the day and satisfy her boss. Back home, the secretaries would be scurrying around with frazzled looks on their faces, coffee beside them energizing them on, as they tried to keep up with their hectic workloads that their demanding bosses pushed on them. What a contrast!

After confirming that the manual *did* include that test, Sergei handed it back to me, and I continued to wait patiently with Lidea. We had a nice chat for a couple of hours, but still, there was no phone call from her boss. We decided to put off the airline ticket arrangements until the following day.

I thanked Lidea for the nice visit (chat) I had with her. I couldn't really thank her for the help she was *supposed* to give me, although she did manage to book me a tentative tour of the Moscow laboratory for tomorrow (which took about thirty seconds of work...and using the phone).

As I was going out the door, I took one last look back at her in farewell, and I smiled. She was sitting there contentedly, in the same position I saw her two hours ago, leaning forward, hands clasped together on her desk, smiling back, waiting patiently.

"Hurry up and wait," as the saying goes!

— * —

On the way back to the hotel, the driver drove through literally forests of trees, tall and beautiful, deciduous and coniferous, lining the roads of Moscow. This truly is a fabulous city. We stopped at some souvenir stands along the wayside for me to peruse. Other than the usual knick-knacks of foreign origin, of which I was not interested, I spotted some Russian dolls, all individually painted, with their famous, or infamous, Russian leaders of the past, including Gorbachev, Lenin, and Stalin. These matryoshka dolls would make great gifts, so I decided to buy a few.

Although these dolls were only one US dollar each, with rubles not accepted, I was leery and had some irrational thought that transactions in a foreign currency were illegal. I had visions of the KGB, or secret service, jumping out from the shadows and arresting me on the spot. In the big cities, including Moscow, there is a black market for US dollars, with many shady characters standing on street corners, willing to exchange their rubles for US dollars. They are willing to pay more than what the banks offer because of the high demand for them, and because the dollar fairs better against the high inflation here. This street currency exchange is technically illegal because local Russians are expected to buy and sell in their own currency. We were told in advance by Alex to stay away from these situations, and do all financial transactions at the banks.

I looked over to the driver, seeking advice, but he seemed unconcerned, as he smoked away on his cigarette, pondering life. I went ahead and concluded the transactions with US dollars. Nobody from the shadows jumped out to arrest me, so I concluded everything was fine. We went back to the hotel, unscathed, with no unmarked cars following us...at least as a far as *I* could tell.

CHAPTER 28
MY LAST DAY IN RUSSIA

Tuesday May 31
Day 35

Most of the second floor of the Radisson Slavyanskaya hotel is taken up by office space, including a pool secretarial service for the many mainstream news companies that stay here. I needed some photocopying and typing done for my draft report, so I went down there this morning and, for a small fee, used their services.

Shortly afterwards, I met up with Sasha and Sergei from the Heerema office, and they took me to the foreign embassy, in another attempt to extend my visa for the summer. This was the last day that it could be done, as my visa expired at midnight. I secretly hoped that it wouldn't go through. I wanted to head home quickly and see the rest of the Stanley Cup finals with my Canucks team playing. I was also desperately homesick. My summer would have been wasted staying at the lab in Obskaya with nothing to do.

Once our visit to the embassy was finished, and, assuming the extension went through, I would visit the laboratory in Moscow at the noontime appointment. At the embassy, Sasha told me to wait in the car, while they made the arrangements. I waited patiently for two hours. Upon returning, they told me they were seventy-seventh in the lineup. When it was finally their turn, they were told to come back tomorrow because they needed more information from Gazprom.

I immediately realized the implications of this. This would not do, because tomorrow I would then be illegally in the country without a valid visa, definitely a no-no. Now I was in scramble mode.

Heeding Bob's advice that if there was any doubt about the extension, I was to cancel the laboratory visit, and get Lidea to arrange an airline ticket for me to get out of Russia. I told the guys in the front of the car to cancel my trip to the laboratory and head back to the hotel, where I would make arrangements to leave.

But, instead of doing what I told them to do, Sasha said, "No," and continued on, looking straight ahead, ignoring me.

At this point, for a brief moment, I had a mischievous James Bond moment come over me (I really did). I had visions that these two characters in the front weren't really with Heerema, but rather, perhaps with the mafia and were taking me to a river to dump me in it and steal my money and valuable Canadian passport.

So, for a moment or two, I humorously sat back, enjoying the moment, and thought quietly to myself, "This is your problem God. You can take care of it. I'm just going to enjoy this for a while."

But, after a couple of seconds, I realized I had to do something about the pickle I was in. I once again told them what I wanted. This time they listened to me and went back to the hotel. I took it that they had simply misunderstood what I was trying to tell them.

At the hotel, after quickly packing my things, my reformed friends drove me back to the Heerema office. There, Money Penny made arrangements for me to flee Russia by the midnight deadline. I didn't realize that M.P. could speak Russian, or that she worked in this part of the world. She could certainly multi-task.

Since her boss was back, the telephone was available and back into play. But communications, and especially telephone connections, are not the greatest in Russia, so Lidea was on and off the phone for the next two hours, trying to connect and reconnect to the KLM ticket office at the airport. I sat there patiently in front of her throughout this time. I was impressed. She could work hard when called upon, in sharp contrast to when I first met her yesterday. But to her defense, she *was* restricted by the non-use of her telephone. She worked feverishly trying to make the connections, but they kept cutting out. Finally, she decided upon a different strategy. She decided to call the Heerema office in Holland and have the secretary there phone the KLM office at the Amsterdam airport to make the arrangements. It worked. My airline ticket was arranged. But, I would have to pick it up at their office on the third floor at the airport rather than simply going to a check-in counter. No problem; at least that's what I thought at this time.

Today, not like yesterday, I could, and did, thank Lidea for her persistent efforts that she made for me. She worked hard. Unfortunately, I didn't have a rose to give her. As I walked out the door, I looked back. There she was, at it again, sitting there contentedly, leaning forward, hands clasped together on her desk, smiling back and waiting. Her job...well done!

I was driven back by Sasha to the Radisson Slavyanskaya hotel. I made arrangements to settle the hotel bill which came out to almost US$2,000 (about CAN$2,700). Included in this cost were the four and a half nights of stay at US$260 per night, room service, and some very expensive, long distance phone calls to Holland to Ard. I used my credit card to pay for this, of which, I would be reimbursed later when I returned to Calgary.

Since the Heerema office was too busy to supply me with a van to take me to the airport, I went down to the front desk to arrange for a taxi. Unfortunately, because I wasn't thinking, I didn't really give them enough warning, so the taxi driver had to break Sasha's speed record in getting me to the airport on time for my departure. It was raining heavily and overcast and the traffic heavy, but by skillfully dodging in and out of cars and pedestrians, roads and sidewalks, he got me there on time, in one piece.

At the airport, I paid the taxi driver and was now faced with the insurmountable problem of trying to shuffle my six suitcases to the third floor where the KLM business office was. That was where I was to pick up my ticket, not at the normal check-in counter on the main floor. I just couldn't dump the luggage anywhere, or it would have been stolen, so I tried to get a cart from the attendant. They cost only about 2,100 rubles, or about $1.30 each, but after searching my pockets, I realized I only had about half that amount. I pleaded and begged with him, but to no avail. He was firm. No discounts. I only wished I had the same fighting skills of the Lufthansa lady agent whom, at this same Domodedova Airport on our incoming trip a few weeks ago, literally fought with, and obtained carts for us. I desperately needed a cart.

As I stood there, weighing my options, trying to figure out what to do next, a tall stranger came up alongside me. In a southern drawl, most likely an American, perhaps Texan, he asked, "Hey Sonny, what's the problem?"

I told him I didn't have enough money for a cart for my luggage. Eyeing my predicament, he paused, then reached into his pocket and fished out a handful of change. He counted it. It came out to the *exact* amount that I needed, not one ruble less or one ruble more. This, in itself, I thought, was a miracle, to have the exact change. And, it wasn't just two or three coins it was a handful of coins.

Even though this incident with the cart seems trivial, and amounted to only about 1,100 rubles or so, it showed me how God is there to provide for us when you least expect it. Nothing is too big or too small for him. I thanked both God and the man profusely. Was he an angel? Who knows? Maybe.

There was one other occasion I would like to mention where I experienced, or strongly sensed, another spiritual dimension. However, this experience came from the other side of the spectrum. This came when I made the decision to be baptized.

One night, after our Pastor Mr. Neil Earle came over to discuss the ceremony procedure, I decided to go for a walk to a nearby park. It was a beautiful June evening, and the flowers and trees were showing off their colors as I walked slowly along the concrete sidewalk, deep in thought.

As I walked, the park area was ahead and to my right. The road was to my left. There was a car parked in front of me, to my left, alongside the sidewalk. There were two people in it, a young man in the driver's seat, and a young woman in the passenger's seat to the right of him and closest to me. They were sitting there not doing anything. As I slowly walked past them, I turned briefly to have a look at them. The woman had her window rolled down. As I looked at her, she returned a heavy stare back to me and in a very deep, husky voice, almost "demonic-like", told me to "F--- off!" Kind of spooky. I walked on, not saying a word, nor stopping. Did I just encounter a demon? I don't know but it certainly adds to the mysteries and fascinations that we face in our daily walk in life.

CHAPTER 29
REFLECTIONS OF RUSSIA –
THE FINAL SUNSET

As I pass through the passport control, one of the two agents scrutinizes my passport, and then scans it over a bright light, perhaps a scanner of sort, looking for some minute detail that will tell them it is counterfeit. He looks over to his partner and shakes his head.

I don't know what this means and I don't really care. All I know is that I am going home and that's all that matters to me. He hands me back my passport, and I follow the rest of the crowd, like cattle going through cattle gates, to the planes that will take us to our various destinations.

There is no pushing or shoving to get on board, like the helicopter trip across the Ob River from Labytnangi to the Salekhard Airport. There is no drama of running onto the tarmac, in an unnamed town, to the plane as it's about to take off. There is no last minute change of plans, like that of the helicopter circling over us at camp Victoria, telling us, "Not today boys," as it headed north without us.

This is just a quiet, unhurried boarding of tourists and business people, foreigners and locals; a mixture of nationalities and classes, all coming together, heading back to their own little worlds. This is my final goodbye, perhaps never to see Russia again; but right now, I can accept that. I want to be back to my world, back to my comfort zone. I am not overly tired, and the few days of rest in Moscow, has recharged me.

As the airline heads west following the sun, it seems to linger and take forever to set, typical of the many *lingering* times I had in Russia. It is a beautiful sunset, with the clouds in the distant horizon aglow in orange.

In a few minutes time, it will be midnight, the official time when my visa expires. Perhaps I will still be in Russian air space, not that it matters. The sun continues to tarry. It's almost as if Russia does not want to see me leave; it wants me to stay as long as possible. As I watch the sun slowly approach the horizon, I am reminded of the camp in the Arctic. Each evening, the sun would try to, but without success, disappear, to rest for the evening, but couldn't, and continued its dance gently around the horizon.

But tonight the dance is over. There is only one direction the sun, along with myself, is going; west...*towards* the horizon, back to its western cycle that I am familiar with, and for me, back to the western world from which I came from. As the sun slowly dips below the horizon, it gives one last brilliant display of orange rays, like lasers, shooting upwards, lighting the sky and clouds as if to say, "I'm not giving up the day to the approaching darkness of night without a fight." But a moment later, it silently vanishes, and gives up. It is gone, and it is now dark. There is no more twenty-four hours of daylight that I once had. The blackness of the night tells me that this is it, and that my Russian adventures are over.

I pull down the flap covering my window, lean back, and close my eyes. I still have a job to do, and my journey is not yet over; but for the next few minutes, my time will be spent on reflections of the wonderful adventures, and misadventures, I had in Russia.

I left the country with less than two hours to spare on my visa on KLM. It was very nice to get out of Russia and begin my trek home. All day today was overcast and rainy, a type of reflective day of my whole trip. As I was flying, it took a long while for the sun to set over the horizon. It lingered for what seemed like forever due to the direction we were going. I thought this symbolized a lot about my Russian journey, which seemed to linger forever.

CHAPTER 30
LEIDEN, HOLLAND

Wednesday June 1
Day 36

After about a three and a half hour flight, the plane landed at the Schiphol Airport in Amsterdam. I was the first one off the plane, and since the security agents were bored and needed something to do, I was taken aside to be their first "customer" for baggage checks. But after partially unzipping the first suitcase, and seeing my parka, he lost interest, waved me to re-zip it, and sent me on my merry way.

Past the security area, I sat quietly, waiting for someone to pick me up. I wasn't overly concerned that nobody was there to greet me right away since the flight was fifteen minutes early. After about twenty minutes, Jim Oswell, and surprisingly, Bob, came to welcome me. I didn't expect the latter, but at the same time, it was nice to see Bob again.

As mentioned earlier, Jim is spending some time here with his wife and family, as he works at the Heerema office here in Leiden. Bob was his usual smiling self, big grin on his face, as he and Jim both welcomed me back. With Jim driving, and Bob in the front, I enjoyed the pleasant forty-minute drive to the Golden Tulip hotel where I'll be staying. It was nice to be back to the western world with all its amenities that I enjoyed. After a few minutes, Bob looked over his shoulder back at me, and with a grin, let me in on why they were late in picking me up. They had some urgent business to attend to at the airport lounge in the form of a beer or two and had forgotten about the time.

Thanks guys. I can really see where your priorities lie. And thanks for wasting twenty minutes of my life, as I sat there waiting. But, in two or three days I should have my report finished and hopefully be able to head for home. I am very happy!

— * —

Today was an incredibly beautiful day of +17C and slightly humid. I took the fifteen minute walk to the Heerema office with Jim Oswell from the hotel this morning. The streets were alive with people on bicycles and very few cars. There were men in suits with briefcases tucked on the bicycle carriers, ladies in dresses, and children, all riding to their adventures for the day. They have red-bricked areas of the street designating bicycle paths only. It's quite a unique country.

At the office, I once again met up with Ard, who introduced me to some of the ladies, including Marian. She is a secretary who will assist me, as I write the report, using a *Word Perfect* document, of which I am not too familiar with. She is a charming lady, in her twenties, and, as most Dutch ladies her age are, is very well built. She enthusiastically shook my hand and smiled. I was to discover later, as I worked across from her, she also has a great sense of humor as, on occasion, I would hear her chortle in that unique Dutch accent of hers at anything she found amusing in her work.

As I settled down to work, typing my draft report, I was happily interrupted many times by ladies from different departments of the company, coming up to introduce themselves and say hello to me. I was enamoured. They were all charming, warm, and quite jovial. Perhaps they hadn't seen a grizzled foreigner, like me, for some time; or perhaps this gave them an excuse to take a break from their work for a few minutes.

Throughout my stay in Holland, I was to find all the Dutch ladies absolutely wonderful; very generous and gracious. As for the men, well, that's a different story. Let's just say I found them the opposite, in terms of their nature and temperament.

But, when I *was* able to get around to working, I had to do a bit of dodging and weaving, like Muhammad Ali. Marian, who sat across from me, kept throwing me liquor-spiked licorice candies as she shared her delights with everyone. Sometimes she would utter a guttural sound, which I took as a soft curse, so I would humorously chide her on occasion. It was a fun and relaxing atmosphere.

At lunchtime, I was given a meal voucher for the cafeteria and headed there for a sandwich and soup. Jim and Bob weren't there, so I just found a table and blended in with the crowd. By the end of the day, most of my rough draft of the report was typed up and only needed some tidying up to do, and to insert the photographs once they got developed.

On the way back to the hotel, I decided to take a scenic walk around this quaint town. It was a pleasant evening as I made my leisurely walk to a park nearby. As I crossed a bridge over a small creek, I saw a windmill close by, characteristic of the many attractions that this country has to offer. Inside the park, a few couples, young and old, were lounging around, soaking up the sun. A young romantic couple were off to one side, cuddling and smooching. A slight smell of marijuana could be detected as I walked past them.

Back at the Golden Tulip hotel, as I walked in, I passed by a huge glass container, like a gigantic fish bowl, sitting on the front desk counter. Instead of goldfish swimming around aimlessly, trying to find their purpose in life, the bowl was filled with a wide assortment of candies, chocolates, and what looked like M&M's. Nearby was a plastic scoop and plastic bags for you to help yourself. How did I miss that last night? I must have been pretty tired. I filled a bag and headed to my room, looking forward to this evening's snack afterwards.

At supper, I was in for a real treat, which I still consider as perhaps the best meal I have ever had in my life. Perhaps, in reminiscence, I was comparing it mostly to the bland meals I just had in Russia. Garnished beautifully was each entrée. Delicate sweet peas, cooked gently, started the meal, followed by a tossed-salad of romaine lettuce, arugula, shredded radish, cucumber, and tomato. Sumptuous chicken, roasted crisply in a juicy herb sauce, alongside mashed potatoes with melted butter and a sprinkling of dill, followed. A ladle of gravy and a side dish of tenderly cooked baby carrots completed the main course.

For dessert, what else could I have, but their world-renowned Dutch ice cream; vanilla ice cream smothered in freshly whipped cream and rich chocolate syrup on top. I was in gourmet heaven!

With no bills to sign to my room number, and a simple thanks to the waiter, I was off to my room to spend the evening sampling some of Hollands finest... their chocolates!

Friday June 3
Day 38

Over the last two days, with the help of Marian and with the addition of my photographs, I worked on, and completed, my report of the laboratory.

Another lady, Jose, from a different department came over this afternoon and chatted with me about arrangements for my final departure for tomorrow, Saturday, to Toronto and then onto Calgary. She asked if I had any preferences to which airline I wanted. I decided to stay with KLM since I have found them to be good.

Bob also popped in a few times to see how the report was going and asked if I wanted to stay a day or so longer for some sight-seeing around the town. Although Leiden is a beautiful city, with lots to see, I was desperately home-sick and wanted to go home. Besides, I wanted to see my Canucks play in the Stanley Cup finals

Bob was finishing his report on the drilling aspect of things as well as the overall program and would be flying out separately when he was done.

I thanked Jose and gave my thanks and goodbye to Marian as well.

As I was leaving, Jim Oswell came up to me and invited me over to his family's place for supper this evening. I obliged. It was nice that he took the time to host me, and for his wife to give me a home-cooked meal.

As Jim drove us to his house, he drove over a bridge overlooking one of the many canals they have here, and slowed down to show me an oddity. In amongst the bulrushes, at the pond's edge, was a white goose sitting there with a group of ducklings surrounding her. She has "ducknapped" them (no, this isn't in reference to Richard Thompson's live album of 2003). Each year, for the past five years, she has been seen going door to door, honking proudly, showing them off and looking for handouts. It is a yearly ritual. No one knows where she gets the ducklings, perhaps they became orphaned, or perhaps, like the pied piper, she leads them astray: very unusual, but humorous.

I met Donna, Jim's wife, and their three children, ranging in age from a few years old to nine or ten. They entertained me warmly, and I was treated to a wonderful home-cooked meal. As Jim travels back and forth, working out of the Leiden and Calgary offices, his family stays here and rents the house.

I saw a different Jim this evening. I always considered him to be a hard-nosed, stubborn type of engineer and selfsame personality. Instead, I now found him to be a friendly, selfless, and generous human being. He and his family, like Roman and Tatyana back at the laboratory, bestowed warmth and kindness to me.

After dinner, as we sat in the living room, a couple of framed photographs on the coffee table caught my attention. One was of Donna, Jim, and their three kids; happy, smiling, posing for the camera, a typical family photograph that you see on everyone's coffee table or fireplace mantel. The other framed photograph was of another type of family, a mixed one of sorts. It was a photograph of the white goose walking proudly ahead of her brood of newly adopted, perhaps so-called, "Ugly ducklings." But they are not ugly to her. And then again, perhaps, it's the mother that's the newly adopted one.

CHAPTER 31
DEPARTURE FOR HOME

Saturday June 4
Day 39

Last night on our drive to Jim and Donna's place, we stopped in briefly at a booth to get my train ticket to Schiphol Airport.

Early this morning, at the hotel, I met Bernie and Andy, two Americans, who are working on the Yamal part of the project. I had breakfast with them. At the checkout counter of the hotel, a business man in a suit and tie noticed my luggage tickets, with their Calgary tags, so he stopped for a chat. He was from Canada too (Ontario), and he too, was checking out after a business trip here. Small world.

After completing my checkout duties, I shuffled my four luggage bags slowly along the cobbled streets to the train station just a few blocks away. The streets were now, once again, teeming with people scurrying around on their bikes. Although I had two less pieces now, with Bob taking his books back, they still totalled in weight of about eighty pounds. Occasionally, a passing bicyclist, usually a woman, would give me an encouraging smile, or utter something to me (which I assumed were polite words), in their Dutch language. The men usually just ignored me.

At the train station, a pretty, well-dressed, suited lady watched me in amusement, as I plodded awkwardly along, like a turtle, humping my luggage up the platform's steps towards her. At the top of the landing, I stopped to catch my breath. Hoping that she spoke English, I asked her if this was the platform to

Schiphol Airport. She *did* speak English, and told me that, "Yes, this *is* the right platform."

With her curiosity aroused, perhaps by my somewhat disheveled appearance I presented her, she queried me as to what exactly I was doing here. I told her of my adventures and misadventures that I had just gone through the past few weeks. She was intrigued, but fascinated at the same time. She had never been to Russia. I chatted with her for about ten minutes and found out she was a flight attendant working with KLM Airlines, heading to the airport as well. After further discussion, I found out she was working on the same flight to Toronto that I was on that afternoon. Pretty cool!

After the short train ride to the airport, I shuffled my suitcases once again out the nearest exit door, trying not to be an obstacle for the people around me, as they scurried about.

After going up the escalators to the main departure area, I checked my luggage in at the KLM ticket counter and headed to the departure lounge. I sat down, and for the one hundredth time on this trip, went through my pockets and small suitcases, reassuring myself at the same time, that all my important documents were still with me. Check and recheck; passport, visa, credit cards, wallet, airline ticket. Yes, they were all there.

Perhaps that is why, even to this day, I have these reoccurring dreams about myself at a hotel, or in an airport, about to catch a plane, and, in a state of confusion, can't find my important documents. Instead, all I find in my suitcases and pockets are nothing but rocks, paperweights, and useless items, typical of those that poor Charlie Brown would get in his candy bag at Halloween. Then, I would sit there, trying to figure out why on earth I brought them with me in the first place. Utter chaos...the story of my life.

So, as I sat there, reassured that my world was just fine, and that everything was in order, I felt this tap on my shoulder. Looking around me, I saw the same Dutch flight attendant that I had met at the train station, walking by, just saying a brief hello to me once again. I smiled and waved back. She was heading off to her pre-departure rituals and routines.

I looked forward to seeing her again on the plane, but, unfortunately, I was in business class, and she was working in the economy class, so I never did see her again. But still, it was nice to have met her, and that gentle reassuring tap on the shoulder was a nice touch.

It's kind of funny how, the two times I have flown KLM Airlines, I had the opportunity to acquaint myself with a stewardess. The other time was on a flight from Amsterdam to either London or Rome, and my seat was up front, next to hers. As we chatted, she mentioned to me that this was her first international flight. All her previous flights were domestic, inside her country. We had been delayed for one hour prior to take off, and she explained to me that, due to high winds from a previous flight, the cargo doors got damaged, and they had trouble closing them; thus, the delay. This was the same year Europe had some of its worst windstorms ever, and we were at the tail end of it.

As we rose to cruising altitude, we hit severe turbulence, the worst I've ever experienced. All the flight attendants, including her, were strapped in tightly. Teatime would have to wait. I looked over to her. Even though, as a flight attendant whom I'm sure had gone through this before, her face was white. She remained focused, staring straight ahead. But, I have to admire them for their courage. When an emergency happens, they are the first ones to sacrifice their lives and make the necessary, quick decisions, often heroic, for the rest of us.

— * —

I am sitting in the Amsterdam Schiphol Airport passenger lounge, writing this diary, waiting to board KLM Royal Dutch Airlines flight 691 to Toronto, Canada. Departure time is 2:45. I wonder when I get back to Calgary, what lies ahead for me. What new adventures are out there? Or perhaps, will I simply sit back and reflect upon the memories I made? Only time will tell.

All I know is that for the past few weeks of my life, I was taken out of my comfort zone...and I enjoyed it. It was a lot of fun.

Live life to the fullest!

EPILOGUE

The flight to Toronto was pleasant and non-eventful. There was lots of legroom, an armchair that reclines, and a little TV, and more than six or seven movies to choose from. The last week has really been great. The time in Moscow and Leiden has been like a holiday (a rest holiday, as I didn't really see too many sights). Even the three days in Leiden, Holland, where essentially I worked all the time doing the report, I enjoyed it immensely because the people were so friendly to me, and Marian helped me with "Word Perfect" and also in typing the data (she also kept throwing me candies), so I was quite happy. And she had that funny Dutch laugh of hers, although one time she swore in Dutch. I could tell by her expression so I scolded her. Today is day 39 of the trip and only one more leg to complete. I am actually well rested, so I am not overly homesick too much anymore. It's almost time to board. Bye.

During the flight home, between Toronto and Calgary, the pilot continually updated us on the first game in the Stanley Cup finals between the Vancouver Canucks and the New York Rangers. Vancouver ended up winning the game 2-1, with Vancouver goalie Kirk McLean being outstanding, kicking out 51 shots (the pilot probably spent most of his time listening or watching the hockey game rather than flying the plane)! Most of us were happy with those results. Of course, Vancouver went on to lose the series in seven games.

My final record against the computer, in chess, was twenty wins, twenty-three losses and two ties. (I was hoping I would end up winning 50% or more!)

Andre, of course, was the easy chess champion of the Arctic Circle.

After abandoning me in Salekhard (Russia), Bob, John, the two Peters, and Ray flew to various destinations, including home. The next day at work, Ray put up a big map of Russia on the lunchroom wall, and put a circle around the town they had last seen me. Beside it, on a yellow sticky note, he put an arrow on it pointing to the town and wrote the words:

"LARRY RITCO R.I.P. [Rest in Peace.]
ABANDONED BY HIS
COLLEAGUES,
SIBERIA
24 MAY 1994"

UPDATE

In 2012, the 1,100 kilometer Bovanenkovo-Ukhta gas trunk line, which includes the crossing of Baydaratskaya Bay, was completed and came online. This section is part of the 4,196 kilometer (2,607 miles) Transnational Yamal-Europe gas pipeline, which runs from the Yamal/Ural area of Russia through Poland, Belarus, and Germany.

The two 1,100 kilometer parallel pipelines, running *above ground*, are 1,420 mm (56 inches) in diameter and have a wall thickness of 27mm (1 inch). The four 71 kilometer, parallel *submerged* pipelines in Baydaratskaya Bay (Baidarata Bay) are 1,219mm (48 inches) in diameter, and are coated in concrete. The pipelines are designed for a working pressure of 11.8mpa (120atm). There are 9 compressor sections on this Bovanenkovo-Ukhta gas trunk line. To avoid the permafrost from melting, the temperature of the gas flowing through the pipeline is kept below -2C. Construction of the submerged section in Baydaratskaya Bay began in 2008 and was completed in 2012.

A second Bovanenkovo-Ukhta gas trunk line (Bovanenkovo-Ukhta 2) was launched in 2012 and brought online in 2017. This also crossed Baydaratskaya Bay, alongside the first ones.

"The submerged crossing under Baidarata Bay proved to be the biggest challenge in the construction of the gas transmission system. Baidarata Bay is marked by unique environmental conditions: despite its shallow depth, it has frequent spells of stormy weather, with complex bottom sediments and frost penetration to the bottom in winter."

www.gazprom.com/about/production/projects/mega-yamal/

Other sources:

www.hydrocarbons-technology.com/projects/
bovanenkovoukhta-gas-trunkline-system/

https://en.wikipedia.org/wiki/Yamal%E2%80%93Europe_pipeline

ACKNOWLEDGMENTS

I would like to thank the following for their assistance in helping make this book possible:

Emerson Ebbett - Thank you for taking the time and effort to proofread this book before it went to print and for being a great friend over the years.

Doris Lancaster - Thank you also for taking the time and effort to proofread this book and offer insightful comments.

Alex Costin - Thank you Alex. If it wasn't for your faith in me and commitment to having me on this project in Russia, I would obviously not have a book to write (unless I wrote about my boring nine-to-five job back in Calgary; which nobody would read). You went out of your way to respect my Christian faith, and did that little extra in ensuring I was accommodated in all aspects.

To the great God and Jesus Christ, I give a big thank you. Thank you for giving me the opportunity to go to Russia, and provide you with a few laughs concerning my adventures and misadventures. But I also thank you for your overall protection, especially in regards to my forbidden walk and not giving a polar bear a free lunch courtesy of me.

APPENDIX A
OVERSEAS TRAVEL LIST

Overseas Travel List:

This overseas travel list is a list that Alex Costin, our Initial logistics coordinator, gave us, as a general guideline to follow, of things to bring with us to Russia.

Passport	Reading books
Visa	Adapter-electrical
SOS insurance policy	Watch-Dual time
Medical certificate	SW Radio
Medical allergy documents	Walkman
Copy of all papers	Tapes
International driver's license	Batteries
Traveler's checks	Playing cards
US$	Flashlight
Rubles	Liter bottle
Money belt	Sunglasses
Camera	Sewing kit
Film	Earplugs
Foreign dictionaries	Drain plug
Language phrase books	Towels
Russian Legends	Thongs (for shower)
Magazines/Digests	Cockroach stuff

Toilet paper

Insect repellent

Hiking boots

Snow boots

Toque

Gloves

Aspirin

Band-Aids

Toilet bag

Nail clippers

Bar soap

Dental floss

Iodine

Deodorant

Gravol

Hand cream

Vaseline

Imodium (Anti-diarrhea)

Preparation H

Multi Vitamins

Nytol

Q-tips

Rolaids

Senekot (laxative)

Polysporin

Syringes

Shampoo & Conditioner

Sunscreen

Thermometer

Kleenex

Vicks

Vitamin C

Mug/spoon

Instant coffee

Flavor Crystals

220-volt element (adapter)

Can opener

Granola bars

Nutribars

Peanuts

Prunes

Trail Mix

Also, not included in the list:

parkas, mukluks, and sleeping bags.

APPENDIX B
FRIENDSHIPS - PAST AND PRESENT

When I look back on all the nights I had with my co-workers, and now considered friends on this trip to Russia, playing crazy rummy, eating Russian hard bread and drinking warm beer, I am reminded of the great many friendships that I've made throughout my life.

The friendships we make are with people whose traits we find akin to our soul.

Sometimes it's the love, kindness, and caring they give us that bonds them to us.

Sometimes it's their sense of humor, their practical jokes, or their mischievous, conniving nature that draws us to them.

Some provide us with hospitality of a social nature and host parties, dinners, and social events.

Yet, some are simply the people whom we just love to hang out with, because you share common interests with them; your pals, buddies, or the tomboys of the opposite sex, if you are a lad.

With each unique set of characteristics that our friends bring to us, we are entertained in one form or another and provided with a healthy change of pace in our otherwise boring lives. For these reasons, I would like to dedicate this section of the book to my friends, but also pass on to you, the reader, the lessons I have learned from them.

— * —

Susan Poffenroth (Celis) epitomizes the first characteristics of love, kindness, and caring. Typical of her Filipino heritage, she cares deeply about family and friends and will go to extremes in helping strangers in need, or to assist a little old lady crossing the street, even if she doesn't want to cross. But, she has a spontaneous and gregarious nature too, that was shown to me in December 1998.

Four of us, Susan, Adele Sanoy, Dan Graham, and I, took advantage of a last minute airline ticket discount for a weekend trip to San Francisco. Walking down the streets of SF, we spotted three well-dressed suited men standing off to the side, one whom was holding an old style Polaroid camera, the kind that releases a photograph which develops as you wait.

The other two men were the objects of the photo shot, standing there, waiting to get their mug shots. We didn't know if they were business executives, movie stars, millionaires, or tourists just like us. Susan, on the spur of the moment, rushes over to them and approaching from behind, puts her arms around their shoulders, much to their amusement. She smiled and all of them looked to the cameraman and said "Cheese." The cameraman, knowing Susan was there, and without skipping a beat, pressed the button and snapped the picture. As Susan was leaving to rejoin us, he yelled out, "Hold on!" He proceeded to pull the Polaroid picture out and handed it to her.

So somewhere in Susan's treasure chest of Polaroid moments lies a photo of that one moment in time, when someone captured, to the merriment of everybody there, an act of her spontaneous and gregarious nature.

Susan in San Francisco

In 1998, although it was late,
we headed to San Fran Bay.
Susan, Adele, Larry, and Dan, all made up the clan,
as we departed happy and gay.

Walking along on the street, two men we would meet,
posing for a photo display.
Without a word, and as quick as a bird,
Susan showed us her playful ways.

She snuck up from behind, and they didn't seem to mind,
as there really was nothing to say.
As the men stood their ground, with Susan's arms wrapped around,
all said "cheese" as the camera clicked away.

As Susan turned about, the man yelled out,
before she had gone too far.
He pulled out the picture, from his Polaroid fixture,
of Susan with the handsome stars.

Today husband Mark, is kept in the dark,
of the picture which Susan finds amusing.
Of two men in suits, ties, and polished boots,
in the arms of his lovely Susan.

— * —

I've known a few pranksters and jokers over the years, but none surprises me more than Len Furlotte. Len, medium height, thin, very conniving, was brought up on the east coast of New Brunswick near Newfoundland, the hub of all Canadian jokes. One prank he pulled off came at our usual Saturday night card games of *Bug Eye* and poker that I usually hosted. Before making his appearance, Len removed one of his lenses from his glasses, hoping nobody noticed it missing at first. Halfway through the game, with a deliberate raising of his finger, as if to adjust his glasses, and hoping everyone would notice, he proceeded to scratch the inside of his eyelid through the open frame, much to the bewilderment and astonishment of us all.

As he joked about it, he gave the excuse that without a lens he was exercising his eye, thus strengthening it. Years later, he came to one of the parties without his glasses, so perhaps the exercises did work after all (or perhaps he forgot to bring them).

Len Forgot

Mr. Len Furlotte, had simply forgot,
as he let a great big cry.
The glasses of Len, was missing a lens,
as he poked himself in the eye.

— * —

If someone's life is in danger and you come and save him or her, or vice versa, they save you, usually you've made a friend for life. I had that (sort of) happen to me one time.

It was at a Sunday afternoon church outing in the early '90s on a canoe trip down the Bow River in Calgary, Canada. The glowing advertisement on the church bulletin board announced this as a "wonderful, safe, family event for the whole family."

I, along with my good friend Dave Smith, signed up, thinking this will be a great adventure. Kirsten H., tall, pretty, very intelligent, dignified, a single lady I might add, also signed up. But then again, maybe I signed up because of her participation.

Everyone brought their picnic lunches and met just north of the city where the church had the prearranged rented canoes, oars, and life jackets. It was a beautiful, sunny summer day. We had three or four to a canoe that included at least one adult and usually one or two kids or teenagers. The church organizers told us to make sure that everything was tied down in case the canoe capsized. "You don't want to lose anything." That announcement in itself should have been a foreshadowing of things to come, but we thought nothing of it. We tied our personal belongings down, but I left my blue Okanagan College jacket loosely beside me, as I might need it if the weather got colder later on.

We took off and floated downstream amongst the dozen or so canoes with one other adult and two kids in my canoe, and Dave, and Kirsten in separate canoes. The next hour or so was time well spent as we drifted leisurely down the river.

But one thing that no one realized at the time was, that the church had rented lake canoes, as opposed to river canoes, and weren't as stable in rapids.

I didn't realize there was a difference. Not that the Bow River has any white-water rapids, but it does have a few small sections of turbulences, and you have to watch out for the bridge abutments.

About an hour into the trip, about fifty yards ahead, we saw a number of canoes having difficulties navigating a particular stretch. A few underlying currents and large underwater rocks were causing the mayhem. One after another, the canoes started getting swamped, and some were capsizing. Quite a few occupants had tumbled out and were trying to hang on and stay with their upside-down canoes as long as possible. So much for that "wonderful, safe, family event," that the church had so innocently described in its advert.

Our canoe slowed down in preparations to take on the survivors. We all had lifejackets on; it was a warm, beautiful day and not too much cause for alarm. We would simply pick them up as we came alongside them.

"Hey, that's Dave," I yelled out, pointing to a canoe a few yards ahead of us that was overturned. "Let's pick him up." I wanted to save my friend.

Dave, mid-fifties, balding, humorous character when he is in a good mood, instead of keeping safe and staying with his canoe, was dog paddling furiously away from it, towards the opposite shore.

"Dave, we're going to pick up," I yelled out, as we paddled towards him. As we approached him, Dave reached out and grabbed hold of the gunwale. By this time he was a bit exhausted, with being a bit out of shape and slightly overweight.

"You guys are overloaded. There is no room for me. I'll swim to shore," he gasped, as he held on, trying to catch his breath. Even though I knew, and we all knew, we were overloaded to start with, I dismissed his concerns.

"No problem," I assured him. "We can take you on. Trust me I know what I'm doing."

We grabbed Dave and hauled his soaking torso on board. Dripping wet and shaking like a dog, he took his shirt off, wrung it out, and started drying himself off. Despite my confidence, our boat was now severely overloaded and lying very low in the water, perhaps only two or three inches above the waterline.

But I still thought we could take on the rapids that had been the misfortune of so many ahead of us. But, I was wrong. We lasted about 30 seconds. When the first wave hit us, we were swamped, the canoe a foot deep in water. When the second wave hit us, about five seconds later, I knew it was all over. That was it. The last words out of my mouth were, "Okay everybody, time to jump out. Hold onto your oars and stay with the canoe."

But Dave wasn't taking orders from anyone this time. After two unofficial baptisms from this church outing in the space of about one minute, the last time I saw him, he was again dog-paddling furiously, lifejacket on and all, in the opposite direction, to the furthest shore. I wasn't able to save my good friend. From my viewpoint, now about one inch above the water surface, I watched him go. I just hoped that his trust in my poor decision-making, about hauling him aboard an already overloaded canoe, wasn't going to affect our long-term friendship.

As the rest of us, now in the water, tried to hold onto the canoe, it quickly overturned. We were now in desperation mode, trying to grab onto any part of the canoe. Not easy when you are struggling to stay afloat, with few hand-grips available, on a slippery, upside-down canoe floating at high speed down the river.

I should have relaxed and let the life jacket keep me afloat, but I'm not a big fan of water and tend to panic, so I ended up wasting a lot of energy floundering about. After a few minutes, I got exhausted, settled down, and let the lifejacket do its job. Once I managed to get a firm grip on the canoe, I looked around to see if the others were still there. They were, alongside the canoe.

I reminded everyone to stay with the canoe and hopefully, with a bit of treading water or swimming, we could direct it to shore or perhaps touch the bottom. But, the river was too deep, so we just stayed put and drifted with the current.

It seemed like we were in that cold water for about an hour, but it was probably only 10 or 15 minutes, when I saw something coming towards us.

A canoe upstream from us was making its way towards us. It was Kirsten, at the front of her canoe, coming to our rescue. Any embarrassing thoughts I had of being at the wrong end of a rescue attempt, I quelled quickly. I didn't care about dignity or pride I just wanted to get out of that now numbing, cold river. I didn't care who rescued me. Still, at the same time, it was quite nice to know that it would be her.

She silently guided her canoe gently and approached us with the same calm, cool demeanor that exemplified her personality, especially when amongst the single guys in church. I tried not to look too pathetic as I struggled to hang onto the side of the canoe. But everybody else was in the same boat as I was (pun only), hanging on for dear life too. I was nearest to her, so I would be the first to be rescued. By this time, I didn't have the energy to say anything to her, and she didn't waste any words either.

With about five yards to go between us and with rescue so near, her eyes were suddenly diverted elsewhere. My blue Okanagan College jacket that had been sitting loosely beside me in the canoe was now in the water, slowly drifting away. It was such a nice jacket!

But Kirsten was now faced with a dilemma. Should she go after it and save my nice jacket, or should she save me (us)? It didn't take her long to make up her mind. She changed course and went after my jacket. And that was the last time I ever saw her...until of course, about half an hour later, when I met up with her, along with all the other survivors, which was everybody, including Dave, at the church campfire on the shore. Almost all of us, including the ladies, but except Kirsten, were semi-clad, as we attempted to dry out our shirts, blouses, and shorts on twigs and branches, as well as dry ourselves out next to the fire.

Our canoe crew eventually reached shallow waters, and we were able to pull the canoe and ourselves to shore to the waiting campfire. As we stood there shivering and shaking around the fire, trying to get warm, I could see the artificial smiles on everybody's faces, as if to say, "Isn't this just a lovely day today? Aren't we having a fun time?"

As we roasted our wieners (pun included) and ate soggy sandwiches, I saw Dave muttering to himself, incoherently, opposite the fire to me. I'm sure he was mostly cussing and cursing us (probably mostly at me, and wondering why he had been deceived into this temptation of a folly of a "great afternoon" of river canoeing). But, as far as I was concerned, Kirsten was there, and that's all that mattered

I had no ill feelings towards her, over her crucial decision she had to make. I just wished it took her longer than just a split second to make her decision between the jacket and me. In addition, she did save my jacket; and she did hand it back to me, although I suppose she might have kept it as bounty in remembrance of the many "Titanics" that were sunk that day. And, did I say, "It was really a nice jacket?"

But we all survived that fateful outing, although most of us looked like drowned rats when we got home. And I believe a divorce was narrowly avoided when a husband and wife team, names withheld, got into a shouting match over her accusations about the *incompetency* of the boat's captain, i.e. her husband, that led to the capsizing of their boat. [Thanks to one of my proof-readers, Emerson, for reminding me of that incident!]

Dave's faith in humankind was eventually restored and we became friends again, although for some reason, we never had any more river canoe trips together.

Kirsten was on one of the few canoes that made it safely through the rapids that day. Perhaps her calm actions in the face of danger, personifies her charac-ter and who she is. As the waves raged on, tossing us "to and fro," she carried on, unflustered, under control, paddling towards us; paddling through the tempest of adversity.

— * —

Unfortunately, I no longer have that Okanagan College jacket, and my friend-ship to Dave has diminished over the years. Kirsten has moved on to eastern Canada I believe and married someone there. All that remains is a distant memory of that canoe trip, one of many playful adventures that we dared to have in our youthful lives.

— * —

Carie is a lady I worked with for a few years that has that bubbly, cheerful nature and makes friends quickly. She has a carefree and happy personality. One day she approached me, sad and despondent.

"What's wrong, Carie," I asked her.

"I'm sad."

"Why?"

"It's because I don't have any friends."

I was taken aback. Here she was, probably the most popular lady in the whole company, and she was telling me she didn't have any friends.

"But everybody knows you. Everybody talks to you. How can you say you don't have any friends?"

"But they all make fun of me," was her sole response. "They're not real friends." She went on to elaborate that she considered me as her only true friend.

I was flattered because I didn't realize my friendship meant so much to her, but at the same time, I felt disheartened. Sometimes the people you think who have the most friends in their lives are really, deep down, the loneliest. It's only a superficial, outward appearance that they try to maintain to hide that loneliness.

Happily, her discouragement didn't last long. Soon afterwards, she met the man of her dreams, married him, and moved to eastern Canada where most of her family were. We kept in touch briefly, and she seemed happy with her new life.

— * —

The queen of all social etiquette and dinners would have to go to my good friend Gay O'Donnell. I spent many delightful afternoons and evenings in the company of Gay as she hosted barbeques, parties, dinners, and entertained many to their hearts content. A delightful person, she has always lavished upon us good food in a warm atmosphere of friendship. Her get-togethers were always first-class. A bouquet of flowers goes to her.

— * —

Pat Tanner is comparable to my rummy friends I have made here in Russia. He shares many common interests with me, especially in sports. Very athletic in nature, he is also very astute with his card playing abilities.

— * —

Just a few more to mention of the many friends I have made over my lifetime would include Adele, Emerson, C.J. (Carol) Pinette, Ray and Sharlene, Penny Clutton, Liz, Ken, and Megan.

I went with Penny, along with three others to Las Vegas one year and had the time of my life. It wasn't because of the sights and sounds of Vegas that I enjoyed so much, it was because I was with my best friends. I don't think Penny realizes how much her friendship meant to me on that trip. That trip wouldn't have been half the fun if she hadn't been there.

Liz and Megan had two mini dachshunds named Sassy and Lawrence whom I instantly fell in love with. Because of them, soon afterwards, I had two pups of my own, which were named Cassie and Henry. Henry was from their litter, and Megan and Liz's dad, Ernie, gave him that name. They lived to the ripe, old ages of 17 and 15 respectively and were great companions to me over those years. I dearly missed them when they departed this world.

— * —

In June 2017, I went back to Calgary to revisit the many friends I have made over the years and reminisce the times we had together. Susan, now married to husband Mark Poffenroth, graciously allowed me to stay at their place for four days, and we had a reunion BBQ that Saturday for 15 or 16 of us.

Our farmer friend Ray Trout and his wife Sharlene (Pinette) were there and plans were made to have another get together the next year in 2018 at their place in Endiang near Drumheller.

Back on January 1st, 2000 at the turn of the century (yes, I know technically you can argue that the turn of the century is January 1st, 2001 but that's beside the point), we buried a time capsule in Ray's (he wasn't married then) dirt basement floor. We went all out in getting the best time capsule available on the market. We went to Walmart and spent $10.00 on a medium-sized metal barrel that held caramelized popcorn.

After eating the popcorn and drinking cold beer in our century ending celebrations the previous night, everyone placed personalized mementos into it. Some of us put newspapers or magazines in it to reflect the current events of the time, while others placed hats, personal items, clothing, or poems or witty sayings. Most of us have since forgotten what we put in, so it will be a blast digging up Ray and Sharlene's floor and turning back the clock 18 years to see what's in it.

Update:

On Sunday July 8, 2018, approximately 6764 days later, the time capsule was dug up. With Pat Tanner doing all the digging, I assisted him greatly, supplying him with bottled water and keeping him hydrated, since it was a hot day. It was hard work. When we entered the dark, dank basement, with its dirt floors, it took us a while to get the lone lightbulb to work. Between me tightening the loose lightbulb and Pat finding the switch on a post, we finally managed. Unfortunately, the switch on the post was not for the lightbulb (the bulb was just loose and needed tightening) it was for the water pump. A couple of hours later, while breakfast was being made, Sharlene let out a shriek telling Ray that there was no water. He went downstairs and turned it on, casting a glare or two in our direction.

It also took us a while to figure out where the capsule was buried, since we couldn't remember. For that matter, I can't remember what I did last week. After finding a large spike and sledgehammer, we probed and found the location. We found the capsule, albeit now with a few holes poked in the lid, and called everyone down.

There were 7 people at this recovery operation. Written on the outside lid of the 5-gallon plastic container that enclosed the Walmart metal popcorn canister, were the words:

Dec. 31, 1999

"THE FRIENDS"

Despite the metal capsule being inside the plastic container, the contents inside were submerged partially in a gooey, watery mess. Initially it was thought this was due to the water tank nearby flooding the floor a few years ago, but upon further evaluation, we think it was from the contents inside. We had a coke can and two beer cans (all full initially) that were rusted out and creating the liquid mess. We found the list that told us there were 10 people at the burial, and what each of us had contributed to the weekend outing. Other than the essential food and snacks, there was a healthy dose (unlike our snacks), of emergency candles and flashlights in case the lights went out and Y2K came to fruition. Ray, the farmer hosting this outing, had a backup cow just in case we had to slaughter it to stay alive over the coming months.

We don't know, or remember what each of us put in the capsule individually, but the items we found inside were: a Reader's Digest, teddy bear, toonie, quarter, Burger King fries wrapper (with fries initially?), Blackwood cigars, champagne bottle, Calgary Herald dated Dec.29, 1999, Buckley's cough drops box (empty-perhaps initially full?), coke can, Kokanee beer can, and a Molson XXX beer can (all the cans partially full).

All the items were in a poor, wet condition. The Calgary Herald and Readers Digest weren't readable. We uncorked the champagne and tasted it. It was a bit flat. I decided to stay with my vodka when we played cards later.

Although we were all happy that Y2K didn't come to fruition (although it might have been fun playing cards in the dark, next to a candle, for a while), I think the one that was most happy was the backup cow.

— * —

Friendships are by far the most important thing in my life, more important than money or wealth. I have never been in need of money. Although my parents weren't rich, they weren't poor either. Whenever I needed financial support, there were always there to help my sisters and me. My friends have made my life richer and more meaningful, and I have been honored by God to have them. With all the traits I have mentioned in this chapter, perhaps the following can simply sum up friendships.

When I was in my early twenties, I lived in a townhouse in Calgary with Dennis Hunt, next door to the landlady and her son and daughter. Many afternoons during the summer months when school was out, Cherie Lynn, in her mid-teens, tall for her age, long blonde hair, would quietly sneak over to my ground floor suite and stick her head in the open, unscreened window. With her curious big blue eyes, she would stand there, watching me in silence, as I typed away at my newly acquired Atari computer and word processor until I noticed her. I think it was often a game to her. When I finally did notice her, her words always started with, "What are you doing?" followed by the custom-ary "Why?" after I answered her first question. Being bored, she would often come over and sit on the windowsill, watching me and asking questions as I typed away. She would continue to watch me on my computer until some of the kids on the large communal lawn would draw her attention, then it was a quick, "See you later," and she was gone.

One day she wanted to print something out, just for the fun of it, on the printer. "Can I print something?"

"Sure."

Without hesitation, she climbed through the window and dropped into the room. She was a tomboy and didn't need doors to get to where she was going.

The printer was old style compared to those of today, with the continuous roll of paper and the much-needed "Lprint" command at the end of your code to get a printout. I showed her how to do it.

After pausing for a moment to think about what she would include, she typed:

FRIENDS
True friends are like
diamonds.
Precious but rare.
False friends are like
autumn leaves.
Found everywhere.
By Cherie L. LaBrash

I don't know if this was her own original poem, or if she got it from somewhere else. Nonetheless, I thought it was pretty cool. I still have that original sheet of paper with her typed poem of "FRIENDS" on it.

"After abandoning me in Salekhard (Russia), Bob, John, the two Peters, and Ray flew to various destinations, including home. The next day at work, Ray put up a big map of Russia on the lunchroom wall, and put a circle around the town they had last seen me. Beside it, on a yellow sticky note, he put an arrow on it pointing to the town and wrote the words:

'LARRY RITCO R.I.P. [Rest in Peace]

ABANDONED BY HIS

COLLEAGUES,

SIBERIA

24 MAY 1994' "

My response to Ray Hunt's premature handwriting on the wall is this:

As Mark Twain once said, "The rumors of my death are greatly exaggerated."

But when the time comes,

my epitaph, albeit humorously modest, would read:

"Larry was a simple man,

who led a simple life."

THE END

ABOUT THE AUTHOR

Larry Ritco's breakthrough from his boring nine-to-five job, and theme of this book, came in 1994 when he was given the opportunity to be part of a six-man observation team and head to northern Russia to the shores of Baydaratskaya Bay.

With an eclectic sense of humor, Ritco writes about his travels, and the "not so funny at the time, but funny now" experiences he had along the way.

Born in Oliver, British Columbia in 1958 and raised in the Okanagan Valley, Ritco decided on a career in Civil Engineering and attend Okanagan College. After spending fourteen years in Calgary doing engineering work, this opportunity came along.

His inspiration to write this book came four years later, in 1998, after talking to his lady friend in High River, Alberta at a local restaurant....It took Ritco only twenty years to follow up on her suggestion and finally write this book!